W9-CXT-445

AMERICAN
THEOLOGY
IN THE
LIBERAL
TRADITION

Books by Lloyd J. Averill
Published by The Westminster Press

AMERICAN THEOLOGY IN THE LIBERAL TRADITION
A STRATEGY FOR THE PROTESTANT COLLEGE

Lloyd J. Averill

AMERICAN THEOLOGY IN THE LIBERAL TRADITION

THE WESTMINSTER PRESS

PHILADELPHIA

Grateful acknowledgment is made to The Macmillan Company for permission to use selections from:

The Heritage of the Reformation, by Wilhelm Pauck. Revised and Enlarged Edition. Copyright © 1961 by The Free Press of Glencoe, Inc.

A Theology for the Social Gospel, by Walter Rauschenbusch. Copyright 1917, by The Macmillan Company; 1945, by Pauline Rauschenbusch.

Library of Congress Catalog Card No. 67-13164

Published by The Westminster Press®
Philadelphia, Pennsylvania

PRINTED IN THE UNITED STATES OF AMERICA

In grateful memory of
Edwin McNeill Poteat
and in present gratitude to
George Lukens Collins
and
Wilbour Eddy Saunders
exemplars par excellence
of the liberal spirit

CONTENTS

PREFACE

The study of American liberal theology that has culminated with this book was undertaken more out of filial gratitude than out of detached historical interest. My own Christian faith, first formed under conservative Baptist influences, might not have survived the critical tests of undergraduate skepticism and military nihilism had it not been for the intellectual and personal ministrations of some distinguished liberal Christians.

Professor Carl Purinton, then of Beloit College and later of Boston University, first opened to me the exciting possibility of a faith untrammeled by doctrinal defensiveness and parochialism. This new influence was prematurely cut off by military service in World War II, during which I went through a period of theological and ethical crisis. Since the intellectual resources of my military surroundings were severely limited, I entered hesitantly into correspondence with several prominent Christian intellectuals known to me only by eminent reputation, in the hope of finding clarity in the midst of my considerable uncertainty. The result was more than I could have hoped for.

Harry Emerson Fosdick was one of these men, and he answered the letters of his young correspondent with the patience, understanding, and Christian wisdom that have helped hundreds through to a firmer faith. He sent me a copy of *The Meaning of Faith,* and later I found *The Modern Use of the Bible* in a U.S.O. library and devoured it with the eagerness and gratitude of a victim of theological famine. Charles Whitney Gilkey, then dean of Rockefeller Chapel at the University of Chicago, was another of my correspondents, and he offered personal friendship to match his intellectual encouragement as we walked the Midway or talked in the study of his Hyde Park home.

Wartime military assignment providentially took me to Madison, Wisconsin, where I became acquainted with George L. Collins, Baptist campus minister at the University of Wisconsin. " Shorty " Collins epitomized the finest features of liberalism — its devoted discipleship in the cause of Jesus of Nazareth and its consequent social passion — and his influence on Wisconsin undergraduates was almost legendary. In the presence of his gentle but incisive example, I found my own faith taking a shape that two succeeding decades have modified but not basically altered. From Wisconsin I went to Colgate Rochester Divinity School, which was the intellectual and institutional inheritor of the theological work of William Newton Clarke and Walter Rauschenbusch. There, too briefly, I fell under the charismatic spell of Edwin McNeill Poteat, surely one of the most original and brilliant preachers of liberalism's later period. There, too, I began my academic career as a very junior instructor under the presidency of Wilbour Eddy Saunders, to whose continued personal and professional encouragement I owe more than friendship can easily repay.

There is nothing unique about this spiritual pilgrimage. Indeed, I dare to recount it here partly because the reader has a right to know what theological predilections are present in and under a work that seeks to be historically objective, but even more because the pilgrimage is common to many members of my own theological generation. We have passed through a strikingly similar experience, from an uninspiring and unpromising conservatism, through the challenges of academic study and of war, to the saving influences of campus ministries and theological seminaries informed by the liberal vision and moved by the liberal passion. We are the beneficiaries of many of the same exemplars of the liberal tradition. We share a common gratitude that changing theological fashions cannot efface.

My own special gratitude is also gladly acknowledged for those who, at various stages since the work on this book was begun ten years ago, have given me the benefit of their criticism. If they do not recognize its influence on the final product, that is not because it was not gratefully received and seriously considered. Profs. William Hamilton, Harmon Holcomb, Winthrop Hudson, and Dean Milton Froyd, teachers and former colleagues at Colgate Rochester Divinity School, have been helpful in many ways throughout the period of writing. Prof. H. Shelton Smith of Duke, Prof. Robert Handy of Union, and Prof. Sidney Mead of Iowa read an early draft of the material contained in Chapters Three and Four. More recent critical readings of the manuscript in its present form were done by Prof. John Spencer, Mr. Spencer Bennett, and Miss Carol Anne White, all of Kalamazoo College.

Finally, appreciation must be expressed to the Danforth Foundation, and especially to its Associate Director, Dr. Robert Rankin, for a grant that made possible a year of study during which this work was begun.

L.J.A.

One PROLOGUE: THE SHAPE OF THINGS PRESENT

A. The Recovery of Liberalism

IN 1932 WHEN Reinhold Niebuhr published *Moral Man and Immoral Society,*[1] Protestant theology in the liberal tradition was clearly on the defensive after almost fifty years during which it had been the ascendant mode of Christian thought in America. Niebuhr's book established the " realistic " school of theology, so called to mark its reaction against the liberal optimism about man and society, and it struck a decisive theological blow at the liberal movement that had already been hard hit by the brutalizing war of the teens, the lurid excesses of the twenties, and the enervating depression of the thirties.

After 1932, the most influential estimates of the character and importance of liberalism were drawn from the polemics of Niebuhr and its other detractors. This is by no means to say that after 1932 liberalism ceased to play a constituent role in American theology. Neo-orthodoxy, as the outlook generally derived from Niebuhr came to be called, was clearly a postliberal development, which is to say that it built upon the assured gains of liberalism and could only be understood properly in its continuity with liberalism. Indeed, a case can be made for the view that neo-orthodoxy retained its original character only in the generation when its chief proponents were men, like Niebuhr, who had once been convinced liberals. The second generation of neo-orthodox theologians, who had never known liberalism at first hand, began to work subtle but significant changes that broke the tension between optimism and pessimism, and between responsible cultural involvement and critical cultural detachment, which had been at the heart of Niebuhr's outlook.

Nor has theological liberalism lacked its own significant voices during the last three decades. Harry Emerson Fosdick reached the height of his pulpit career in the Riverside Church and the widest extent of his national audience through radio and writing precisely during that period. Other nationally prominent preachers — Ralph Sockman, Bernard Clausen, Charles Whitney Gilkey, Edwin McNeill Poteat, and Ernest Fremont Tittle, to name only a few — were spokesmen for the liberal movement. In the seminaries, respected theologians such as Robert L. Calhoun of Yale, John Bennett of Union, L. Harold DeWolf of Boston, Walter Marshall Horton of Oberlin, Bernard E. Meland and Daniel Day Williams of Chicago reworked the mainstream of social and theological liberalism. If all this activity belied the popular notion that liberalism was dead, crushed by the combined weight of neo-orthodox polemic and historical catastrophe, it was still true that from the 1930's to the 1950's the liberal movement was in serious decline if not in actual disrepute. The pulpit lags behind theological trends and gives a misleading impression of the real vitality of what appears to be the predominant mood of the moment. It is interesting that the American pulpit experienced a decline after the passing of the generation of liberal preachers whose representatives were named above. The fact that there were few, if any, successors in that line of national pulpit figures is evidence for the change that had been building up at the precise time when those men appeared to be at the height of their professional influence. It also suggests that, respected as some liberal teachers of theology were, their own theological work was increasingly isolated in the general community of academic theology and that, consequently, their influence on the next generation of preachers was seriously limited.

It is notoriously difficult to locate with any precision the end of one intellectual movement and the beginning of another, and in the present case it may be wise to content ourselves with the essentially modest claim that, in the decade following the end of

World War II, liberalism began to reassert itself as a growing theological force on the American scene. And if it was now a liberalism refracted through two decades of ruthless and relentless theological criticism and chastened by those almost incredible events that immediately surrounded the opening of the nuclear age, it was, nevertheless, a liberalism in identifiable and self-conscious continuity with that older movement which had first taken shape in the last two decades of the nineteenth century.

In 1950, University of Chicago church historian Wilhelm Pauck, who had been an early American interpreter of Karl Barth, recorded his judgment that

> a renaissance of theology is taking place in contemporary Protestantism. It does not yet affect the churches in such a way that older theological attitudes and views are replaced and that a new Christian outlook upon the world is determining the work of the churches. To be sure, such tendencies do manifest themselves, but they have not yet gained decisive power.[2]

Decisive or not, the shape of things to come was clear to Pauck. Looking beyond the immediate postwar period in which he wrote, Pauck predicted that " the church of the future must and will be liberal." [3] Indeed, he saw that recovery already beginning to take shape in a new school of "radical theological liberalism"; [4] and in this observation he anticipated the emphasis on a secular Christianity and a "theology of the death of God" that was reaching the climax of its public notoriety some fifteen years later. The radicalism of the new liberals, in Pauck's view, lay in their rejection of the church as the context for their work of theological reformulation, and in their definition of " the religious attitude of modern man upon the basis of the scientific interpretations of the universe, in dependence upon the new biological, psychological, and sociological knowledge of man, or in terms of the modern philosophy and history of religion." [5] The older liberals, said Pauck, had been primarily churchmen who sought, within the existing ecclesiastical structures, to find fresh ways to express the abiding truths of the Christian revelation; but the new radicals had no interest in serving the churches and addressed themselves, instead, to secular men alienated from the Christian tradition but seeking guidance for the complex business of living. Because of their deliberate separation from the Christian community in its historical and contemporary forms, in their search for authentic faith, the radicals had substituted philosophical norms for historical norms and had thus fallen into what Pauck called "a modern form of the mystical [i.e., nonhistorical] approach to religion." [6] But mysticism has been durable and effective, Pauck insisted, only when it has been "grafted upon historical religions." [7] Thus, ironically, its neglect of the historic Christian community would inevitably bring about the demise of the new radicalism.

In the place of a radicalism deficient because it scorns the historical tradition of the gospel, and equally in the place of a neo-orthodoxy that is in danger of taking the tradition so seriously as to substitute it for the gospel, Pauck called for a new ecumenical theology combining the radical insistence upon contemporaneity with the neo-orthodox insistence upon the uniqueness of the gospel.

In our day it is much easier for theologians to work in the spirit of ecumenical theology than it has ever been before. The historical understanding of the Christian religion has liberated them from that orthodoxy which was bound to the literally inspired Bible, to authoritarian creeds, and to other unchangeable norms. It has enabled them to see that the Christian gospel can be comprehended only in and through pluralistic historical forms and that the Christian faith cannot be anything else but that dynamic response to the divine call in Jesus Christ which comes to individual men and groups of believers only through the media of many historical forms of Christian faith and order, life and work. The theological interpreters of Christianity cannot do their work except on the basis of historical and comparative theology. They are thus required to practice an open-mindedness that makes them willing to listen to all serious interpretations of the Christian religion.[8]

The distinctive legacy of liberalism, in Pauck's view, was its insistence on the historical character of the gospel; and the passion for theological contemporaneity that was so characteristic of the liberal outlook was precisely the product of this historical awareness.

The great theological movements of Liberalism and Modernism have compelled [the Protestant church] to recognize new fields of duties toward the modern age. The tremendous work of the historical criticism of Christian tradition has returned to history what belongs to history. Thereby, the liberal school has given us understanding and perspective. . . . The group of Christians whom we call modernists have taught us to accept the challenge of the modern day and, free from the authority of tradition, have begun to interpret Christianity in terms of the requirements of modern life and knowledge. In so far as modernism leads to the concrete duty of taking our own historical situation seriously, the church of the future must be Modernist. With the help of the critical methods of theological liberalism and of the constructive attempts of Christian Modernism, we are charged to build a Protestant Christianity which cultivates *Wirklichkeitsreligion.*[9]

Similarly, it is the historical character of the gospel which requires that the new theology be ecumenical theology.

As the various denominations and churches are brought into close touch with one another, they are forced to recognize that they hold the eternal gospel in temporary historical forms. They are thus compelled to seek a confrontation with the gospel itself, so that they may develop a loyalty to the divinely creative core of Christianity and not to its perishable human conventions. But this gospel is available only in historical man-made traditions. It must therefore be sought *in* them and not *apart* from them. This is why the activities of the ecumenical and interdenominational organizations are so important.[10]

It is significant for our interest in the changing postwar theological mood that Pauck's book, first published in 1950, was revised and reissued in 1961 [11] with his predictions concerning the recovery of liberalism unchanged. Indeed, if anything, it would seem that the intervening decade had strengthened his conviction about the need for a new liberalism. The revisions in the 1961 edition consisted primarily of the addition of critical chapters on the work of Adolf von Harnack and Karl Barth. Harnack's great contribution to Christian scholarship was not what he added to the store of historical knowledge but simply " his insistence that Christianity must be understood as a historical movement and that it must be interpreted by the historical method." In Pauck's comparison of these two giants of Christian intellect, his preference was clear:

> Today, the human situation, including that of the churches, must be handled by critical anthropological thinking and by means of decisions derived from clear, judicious historical thinking. Barth says that church history is merely an auxiliary theological discipline, because he believes that the church must be guided by dogmatic theology oriented in the Bible. But dogmatic speculation, even if it is based on the Bible, cannot help us. What we need most is historical understanding and not theosophy. The churches have more need of a Harnack than of a Barth.[12]

Three years before Pauck's book first appeared, his Chicago colleague Daniel Day Williams had given the Rauschenbusch Lectures at Colgate Rochester Divinity School. In his choice of a theme for the lectures, Williams had been moved by the conviction that " the need is imperative for a restatement of the Christian doctrine of man and his historical destiny." [13] The problem that contemporary history has thrust upon us, he wrote, is one of finding an adequate Christian interpretation of human progress,

> recognizing that it is not so simple a problem as romantic idealism made it, nor yet so simple as the present somewhat contemptuous rejections of it suggest. We must try to find a more compelling expression of the Christian conviction that faith and hope and love are the abiding realities which sustain the human spirit within and beyond the fates of individuals and civilizations.[14]

The thesis Williams sought to defend and illustrate was that contemporary Protestants "*are not forced to make a simple choice between liberalism and neo-orthodoxy,*" and that, in fact, both schools are deficient because " they have no place for God's *redemptive* work in human history." [15] But if in his own theological construction Williams sought to go beyond both schools, he was, nevertheless, prepared to acknowledge that his own position placed him " within the tradition of the Christian social gospel of which Walter Rauschenbusch was both prophet and pioneer."[16] That this acknowledgment was no merely formal nod in the direction of the one in whose honor the lectureship had been endowed is shown by a reading of the lectures, published in 1949 under the title *God's Grace and Man's Hope*. In any event, it was clear to Williams that the required new theological construction called for a faithful historical recovery of the older liberalism, even as it sought to go beyond that liberalism.

When, in 1959, L. Harold DeWolf wrote *The Case for Theology in the Liberal Perspective*,[17] he did so, he said, because of the rather strident character that had overtaken neo-orthodoxy — an antiliberal mood which DeWolf found difficult to distinguish from fundamentalism in its more bellicose and barren forms. "There is need," he wrote, "to sound again the positive notes that were contributed by the older liberals at their best, and to show their relevance to the historic Christian faith."[18]

Pauck, Williams, and DeWolf were by no means the only instances of a changing emphasis in American theology during the postwar years, but they were distinguished representatives of a slowly gathering conviction that liberalism deserves thoughtful reappraisal, and that such reappraisal can take place only in the presence of a careful historical reconstruction of the liberal movement.

The most substantial work of historical recovery yet to appear is Kenneth Cauthen's *The Impact of American Religious Liberalism*.[19] Cauthen's survey covers the period 1900–1930 and examines in some detail the theological contributions to liberalism of William Adams Brown, Harry Emerson Fosdick, Walter Rauschenbusch, A. C. Knudson, Eugene W. Lyman, Shailer Mathews, D. C. Macintosh, and Henry Nelson Wieman. "Those who, like the author, grew up being told that liberalism was a bad word," Cauthen wrote,

> may profit from a comprehensive survey of liberal thought presented through the writings of the greatest, or at least the most representative, exponents of the outlook. . . . There is need for all sides to re-examine this version of the faith which once saved many from unbelief or agnosticism.[20]

More than that, Cauthen believed his survey would serve a prospective as well as a retrospective purpose, since

> much of the structure of liberalism has been carried over into those theologies which have been most critical of liberalism. Those who rebelled against liberalism in the thirties and forties of this century were very conscious of their points of disagreement with liberal thought, but they perhaps did not break as fully with this perspective as they may have believed at the time. There are important continuities as well as discontinuities between liberalism and post-liberal theology, making it incorrect to speak of liberalism simply in the past tense. To what extent are liberalism and neo-orthodoxy basically alike despite certain fundamental differences? This is a question which needs attention at the present time, particularly as we begin to think about the direction in which American theology needs to move in the future.[21]

If the intellectual work of any historical period is to be recovered and reassessed, there must be ready access to the writing of that period. During the past decade, inexpensive editions have appeared of some of the most important works for an understanding of the liberal movement: Schleiermacher's *On Religion: Speeches to Its Cultured Despisers* [22] and *The Christian Faith;* [23] Harnack's *What Is Christianity?* [24] *The History of Dogma,*[25] and *The Mission and Expansion of Christianity in the First Three Centuries;* [26] and Troeltsch's *Christian Thought,*[27] *Protestantism and Progress,*[28] and *The Social Teaching of the Christian Churches.*[29] The Library of Protestant Thought has produced edited texts and introductions to other significant figures such as I. A. Dorner,[30] Horace Bushnell,[31] Washington Gladden, Richard Ely, and Walter Rauschenbusch.[32] Ritschl's *The Christian Doctrine of Justification and Reconciliation,* long out of print and almost impossible to find, is now being offered by a reprint publisher.[33]

Serious and substantial studies of individual theologians are giving depth to the broader surveys. An objective reassessment of *Schleiermacher on Christ and Religion* [34] appeared in 1964; the thought of Ernst Troeltsch has been newly examined under the title *Toward a Theology of Involvement;* [35] and a major publisher is offering a series on Makers of Modern Theology with similarly serious studies of Ritschl, F. C. Baur, Schleiermacher, and Harnack.[36]

The fact that a public already exists for these works is itself evidence of a fresh interest in liberal theology, and reflexively, the easy availability of these works is likely to extend that public and intensify its interest.

Rudolf Bultmann's words in his introduction to the 1957 edition of Harnack's *What Is Christianity?* may be taken to summarize much of the motivation for this growing attention to an older tradition, both by those who share it and by those who stand outside of it. After suggesting that Harnack's book should be read today for the simple reason that it is "a theological-historical document of the greatest importance," Bultmann adds:

> The young theologian may also learn something else from this book; namely, what conceptions of Christianity he may presuppose to be current among the broad circles of the educated and semi-educated laymen to whom he must address his sermons and teachings. There is no doubt that the popular understanding of the Christian faith . . . accords in some measure with the portrait drawn by Harnack, even if it does not achieve his earnestness and subtlety. But it should also be stressed that this understanding of Christianity, although one may label it "liberal," is in no wise a lifeless residue of a vanished era which no longer needs to be taken seriously. On the contrary this "liberal" understanding, at the very least, contains active impulses which though now obscured nonetheless preserve their legitimacy and will recover their validity.
>
> During a discussion on Protestant religious instruction, . . . Rudolph Lennert, in an open letter to Helmut Kittel, declared that "theologians, even perhaps in their own interests, must arrange to come to terms with these old concerns of liberal theology and in a manner somewhat more serious than they show today. For unless all signs are deceiving, these concerns will present themselves afresh to theologians with a new vigor, and with a new radicalism, as though strengthened by their long response." One might also properly point out to those who would simply dismiss theological liberalism as a "false doctrine" that there is no heresy whose motivation and strength do not spring from a valid impulse that fails to achieve legitimate expression in the official "true doctrine," even when it

seeks to wrest this acknowledgement of its worth by taking the path of error.[37]

So the evidence has been growing for some time that the next major development in American theology will center in the recovery of a liberalism which has been refracted through the theological and cultural experience of the last thirty years. Unrepentant and unreconstructed liberals will call this recovery historical justice, but they should not be too ready to gloat. If they find a certain thrill in reading again the confident theology of a Rauschenbusch or a Mathews, they will also recognize, perhaps a little sadly, how much those men said which can never be said again.

Unrepentant and unreconstructed " realists " will call this recovery a retreat, but they would do better to understand why it is that liberalism now reasserts itself. If the movement of theological " realism," which centered in Niebuhr, is now unable to perpetuate itself, that is probably because it has become the possession of a generation of advocates to whom the liberal movement is essentially foreign and whose " realism," as a consequence, has in many instances become little more than a capitulation to an uncritical cultural cynicism scarcely more satisfactory than the liberal's earlier capitulation to an uncritical cultural optimism.

It is to the work of objective historical reexamination of American theology in the liberal tradition that this present essay is intended as a contribution. Its chief purpose is to permit the liberals to speak for themselves. For this reason, in the major sections of the book direct quotations are employed as often as the clarity and continuity of the text permits, while the critical observations of the author are restricted to the Prologue and Epilogue.

B. Historical Limits

Darwinism, both biological and social, is the key to the *terminus a quo* of Protestant liberalism in America. The pages that follow will substantiate Daniel Day Williams' definition of " liberal theology " as " the movement in modern Protestantism which during the nineteenth century tried to bring Christian thought into organic unity with the evolutionary world view, the movements for social reconstruction, and the expectations of ' a better world ' which dominated the general mind." [38] Evidence for the definitive influence of evolution and its attendant social optimism is supplied by the fact that, *in the profile of liberalism which is given in Chapter Three, every one of the characteristics listed has an evolutionary reference,* either directly or indirectly.

While it is certainly true that elements in a developmental world view were being supplied by philosophy and science during the century before Darwin, it is also true that Darwin's work had the effect of focusing those evolutionary predilections and investing them with peculiar empirical and intellectual force.

The Origin of Species appeared in 1859, and within two decades it had begun to give shape to a theological movement. The influence of Darwinism first came to explicit expression in the so-called New Theology, that school which appeared in the last quarter of the nineteenth century and which numbered among its adherents such figures as Theodore Munger, Newman Smyth, George Gordon, Washington Gladden, William Newton Clarke, and William Adams Brown. The first forthright statement from this group on the issue seems to have been Newman Smyth's *Old Faiths in New Light.*[39] Published in 1879, this was the first in a series of studies in which Smyth attempted to adjust theology to Darwin's theory of evolution as well as to the new Biblical criticism. Smyth had become so fascinated with the developments in biological science that he took time off from his pastorate in New Haven to do his own experimental work in the laboratory at Yale.[40] In a reminiscence near the end of his life, Smyth confessed that experimental interests came to replace dogmatic theology as his major preoccupation:

The . . . thirst for the real led me away somewhat from the field of theological studies in the endeavor to find what could be known, how near towards ultimates we might come through scientific researches. The early fruits of these inquiries in what has now become the voluminous department of physiological psychology, were then accessible and a better understanding of Darwinism was becoming prevalent in Christian apologetics. These recent investigations and every advance of science towards the origin of things, every ascertained fact far out on the border line between the known and the unknown, had for me a fascinating attraction, as indeed pursuit of spiritual truth in this direction has been to me since — much more than dogmatic theology — my chief study and delight.[41]

In an essay in definition of the movement written in 1883, Theodore Munger explained that the New Theology

justifies itself by the belief that it can minister to faith, and by a conviction that the total thought of an age ought to have the greatest possible unity, or, in plainer phrase, that its creed ought not to antagonize its knowledge.[42]

This meant, clearly, that one of the chief tasks of theology was to seek rapprochement with science; and indeed, one of the positive features of the New Theology, as Munger described it, was

a new relation to natural science; but only in the respect that it ignores the long apparent antagonism between the kingdoms of faith and of natural law,— an antagonism that cannot, from the nature of things, have a basis in reality.[43]

So H. Shelton Smith, in his study of the New Theology, wrote that

as a group they took seriously (though not uncritically) the Darwinian theory of evolution, and they endeavored to harmonize their theological conceptions with that theory as fully as possible consistent with maintaining the essential elements of the Christian faith. They did not sanction Darwin's theory of the survival of the fittest, nor did they accept his doctrine of evolution save on theistic premises. But they saw in the doctrine of evolution, as thus qualified, an important truth which had to be taken into account by modern theology.[44]

It is the view taken in this study, therefore, that the formative influence of the evolutionary outlook was such that, before the impact of Darwinism, theological liberalism cannot properly be said to have appeared, however much other elements in the liberal profile may be present. The beginning of liberalism is, therefore, dated at 1879 with the appearance of Newman Smyth's *Old Faiths in New Light.*

If the world was a different world after 1859, it was never the same world after 1918. A liberal Protestant journal, which had been founded in 1884, was renamed in 1900, in prophetic expectation that the twentieth century would be "The Christian Century." But after the "Great War" a scant two decades later, there would be few to sing, as Ozora Davis had in 1909:

> At length there dawns the glorious day
> By prophets long foretold;
> At length the chorus clearer grows
> That shepherds heard of old.
> The day of dawning brotherhood
> Breaks on our eager eyes,
> And human hatreds flee before
> The radiant eastern skies.

The radiance of the eastern skies was blotted out by the clouds of war, and human hatreds, which earlier had seemed to be in flight, were found to be in aggressive countermarch. World War I struck a shattering and shuddering blow to the optimism and idealism of the liberal movement. Many pacifists, like Walter Rauschenbusch, felt the sickening impact of war on a scope unprecedented in history. The human brutality of bombings and battlefield carnage, and of atrocities visited upon civilian populations, gave glaring and frightening exposure to a permanent truth about human nature that many had preferred to think was an evolutionary lag soon to be outgrown. Looking back upon those events twenty years later, Shailer Mathews wrote in his autobiography:

> The outbreak of war in 1914 shattered all optimism. Human nature was still untamed. A state could command the loyalty of its subjects in the face of interests that extended beyond the frontiers. It is easy now to be contemptuous of the optimism of pre-war liberalism but when one recalls the elements of the world situation it is not strange that we should have suffered from illusion. Socialism, international labor movements, international commerce, international science, the

Roman Catholic Church, Protestant Christianity, peace societies, the mixture of populations, common culture, all seemed to insure the maintenance of peace. The outbreak of war did more than excite horror for itself. It argued a breakdown of forces which we believed were shaping up a new world order.[45]

Even those who had found it possible to give the war effort their idealistic support as a crusade " to make the world safe for democracy," and whose idealism found fleeting expression in President Wilson's Fourteen Points, fell into disillusionment as a result of the reception accorded Wilson's program, the harsh repressiveness of the Versailles treaty, and the subsequent American refusal to join the League of Nations.

Perhaps the last great statement of the liberal position before the deluge was *A Theology for the Social Gospel* by Walter Rauschenbusch, which appeared in 1917.[46] Its author died the following year. After Rauschenbusch, the liberals became increasingly defensive, besieged as they were by a newly militant fundamentalism and by growing theological discontent within their own ranks.

This is not to say that liberalism ended with World War I. We have already seen how its influence persisted on into the thirties and forties. It is to say, however, that liberalism's effective dominance of American religion was ended by the war; that the postwar liberals were of a distinctly different temper from their prewar predecessors; and that, in spite of attempts to adjust its outlook to a world of war, of temporary and dazzling prosperity and excess, and of sudden depression, liberalism could not save itself. With the appearance of Niebuhr's *Moral Man and Immoral Society* in 1932, the process of theological deterioration, which had begun with the war, reached its climax, and a new postliberal theological era was firmly established in America.

Liberalism in full flower thus belongs to the period between Newman Smyth's *Old Faiths in New Light* and Walter Rauschenbusch's *A Theology for the Social Gospel,* and these are the historical limits that define the present study.

C. A Methodological Problem

Liberalism was a movement in American Protestant thought. Like any intellectual and social movement, it is difficult to delineate without distortion. Donald Baillie has explained [47] analogically the situation out of which paradoxical statement arises in theology by pointing to the difficulties encountered in reducing a three-dimensional system to two dimensions, such as when the spheroid earth is reduced to a map. Any given point on the sphere both is, and is not, located where it appears to be on the map; and it is necessary to employ a device, such as Mercator projection, in order to take account of the ambiguity. A quite similar predicament is involved in the attempt to crowd a movement into a typology. Any given figure in the liberal movement both is, and is not, located by the profile that will be drawn in Chapter Three. He is, in the sense that the total profile which is given there describes a kind of theological locus, " the assemblage of all possible positions of the moving or generating element," [48] within which his concrete position is taken up. He is not, in the sense that any given element within the profile may say either too much or too little to characterize his concrete position accurately. The profile will be useful, then, in abstracting a set of family resemblances by means of which we can relate a man to his theological kin, but it will not tell us in advance what any given member of the family will look like.

Perhaps this methodological issue is important enough to specify some of the assumptions that underlie the present study. In constructing a definition of American theology in the liberal tradition by means of the profile in Chapter Three, it is assumed that it is not necessary to omit from that profile characteristics which may apply as well to other movements. That is, to be capable of independent definition, a movement does not need to be described only in terms of characteristics that are historically unique to that movement. There is probably no such thing as radical historical uniqueness; that is, there are no ideas or events without contributory antecedents. But more than that, the character of a movement is to be found, at least in part, in the way in which it uses and recombines and transfuses elements which it appropriates from other traditions.

A second assumption is that, in constructing such a definition, it is not necessary to delineate a profile against which no exceptions can be brought. Definitions which are built upon only the barest minimum run the danger that what they define will be of little significance. Furthermore, when the subject of definition is a historical movement, the fluid and richly varied state of the movement as a whole makes it virtually impossible to define it in such a way that no exception, from some part of the movement or some phase of an individual's development within the movement, can be brought.

A third assumption is that, in order to identify a given individual as standing within the movement, it is not necessary to establish his entire and detailed conformity with every aspect of the movement, but rather his adoption of a significant configuration of those characteristics which comprise the movement. " Significant configuration " is, of course, imprecise and points to the subjective element that is inevitably involved in judging the appropriateness of locating any given individual within the movement.

Only a single exception to this last assumption has been allowed in the present study, and that is that no theologian is identified as falling within the liberal school who does not share an evolutionary outlook.

H. Richard Niebuhr's comments concerning typology in *Christ and Culture* summarize very well the attitude of this present study:

A type is always something of a construct, even when it has not been constructed prior to long study of many historic individuals and movements. When one returns from the hypothetical scheme to the rich complexity of individual events, it is evident at once that no person or group ever conforms completely to a type. Each historical figure will show characteristics that are more reminiscent of some other family than the one by whose name he has been called, or traits will appear that seem wholly unique and individual. The method of typology, however, though historically inadequate, has the advantage of calling to attention the continuity and significance of the great *motifs* that appear and reappear in the long wrestling of Christians with their enduring problem.[49]

To paraphrase Niebuhr's conclusion of the matter, typology such as that undertaken in this present study may help us to gain orientation as we, in our own time, address ourselves to the same issues addressed by earnest Christians of liberal persuasion in an earlier period.

Two LIBERALISM'S THEOLOGICAL HERITAGE: A BRIEF SURVEY

A. The German Theologians

THE REVERENT view of German scholarship, widely held both in England and in America during the nineteenth century, was aptly expressed in 1857 by Oxford don Mark Pattison:

> It must not be supposed . . . that German Theology is some obscure national product, the concern exclusively of the country which has given it birth. It is no insulated phenomenon. Though generated in Germany, it belongs to Christendom. It is the theological movement of the age. It is only because there is fuller intellectual life in Germany than elsewhere . . . that German characteristics are impressed on the substance of the Christian science. The capital of learning is in the hands of Germans, and theirs has been the enterprise which has directed it into theological channels.[1]

The eminent Scottish theologian Hugh Ross Mackintosh has suggested that German theological leadership in the nineteenth century was probably traceable to (1) the unusually large number of scholars engaged in theological work, staffing twenty-five full faculties, (2) an unusual measure of doctrinal freedom in spite of close church-state relations, and (3) the traditional German love of exact scholarship.[2]

However that may be, there can be no doubt that German theologians set many of the terms for American theological construction and debate in the last century as well as our own. It is at least symbolically significant for the influence of German thought on American liberalism that the figures who begin and end the period presently under examination both studied in Germany. In 1868 Newman Smyth went to Berlin, where he fell under the fascination of Isaak August Dorner, whose own theological position had been markedly influenced by Schleiermacher. Evidence that Schleiermacher's cast of thought shaped Smyth's theological perceptions, whether directly or indirectly, is found in the following quotation from *Old Faiths in New Light:*

> The deeper into the secrets of nature we pierce, the farther back toward the beginning of creation we penetrate, the nearer we are brought to the old mystery of a reality beyond all knowledge, before whose presence and power our imaginations must drop their last images of things, and reason must give place to faith. We feel our dependence upon the Infinite God around us. Faith is the sense of the pressure upon our being of the Infinite Being in whom we live. . . . Beyond the last conceivable subdivision of matter, beneath the last imaginable centre of force, is the One substance — the continuous, indivisible, spiritual ground of existence, the living God.[3]

In Germany, Smyth was introduced to "Biblical theology," and in 1918, he wrote of that new discovery:

> I had never before heard of any such title or method of investigation throughout my proof-text period of education and revolt at Andover. I had been taught how New England theology, plus the Princeton theology, was regarded by the prophets and apostles. I had heard nothing of Biblical theology. It opened to me a new lead, which I hastened to follow. The guideposts along the way were then marked by German signs, and for a few years my theological education had to be entrusted to German scholarship and leadership. Now, one need not go abroad to find out what critical Biblical theology may mean.[4]

If that was true, it was because Smyth and others who had studied the German theologians at first hand had been making their thought popularly available through writing, teaching, and preaching. In 1883 Smyth edited, with introduction and notes, the eschatological sections of Dorner's *Glaubenslehre* under the title of *Dorner on the Future State,* thus making a further contribution to the dissemination of German theological influence on the American scene.

Young Walter Rauschenbusch went from the Rochester Free Academy to the Evangelical Gymnasium of Gütersloh in 1879, and in 1883, after a period of European travel, he enrolled at the University of Berlin for a time before returning to Rochester to complete his undergraduate course and begin his seminary studies. In 1891, Rauschenbusch returned to Germany, this time to study New Testament and sociology at the library in Berlin, and it was also on this trip that he worked on the first draft of *Christianity and the Social Crisis,* perhaps his most influential book. Adolf von Harnack, with Wilhelm Herrmann the most prominent exponent of the Ritschlian school of theology, was teaching at Berlin in that latter year.[5] Donovan Smucker, in his study of Rauschenbusch, notes that Harnack was the author most quoted in the Rochester theologian's books, and that the Ritschlian theology, especially its solidaristic view of sin and the ethical importance it attaches to the Kingdom of God, laid the theological foundations for Rauschenbusch's work.[6] Rauschenbusch himself placed Ritschl at the head of the line of German thinkers, though he found Ritschl finally unsatisfactory because of Ritschl's lack of sociological awareness.

> Kant first recognized the importance of the Kingdom of God for ethics [Rauschenbusch wrote in *A Theology for the Social Gospel*]. Schleiermacher first applied the teleological quality of Christianity to the definition of its nature, but he still treated now of personal redemption and now of the Kingdom of God, without adequately working out their connection. Ritschl has done more than any one else to put the idea to the front in German theology. . . .[7]

Furthermore, as Smucker asserts, the American theologians best known to Rauschenbusch were also Ritschlians who tended to "confirm the general trend of his theology." [8]

Rauschenbusch has been called " liberalism's greatest prophet," and William Adams Brown has been called " liberalism's most eminent teacher." [9] Brown was a student at the University of Berlin from 1890 to 1892, arriving the same year that Harnack took up his professorship in the University. Kenneth Cauthen denominates Brown a " neo-Ritschlian," since " in his definition of Christianity, in his grounding of religion in the practical reason, and in his emphasis on historical revelation . . .

Brown followed the familiar lines laid down by Ritschl." [10] Shailer Mathews was also at the University of Berlin in 1890, and though he studied history and political economy rather than theology, the experience was as formative for him as for his theological colleagues. " So far removed was I from the field of theology," Mathews later boasted,

> that I never heard even so distinguished a man as Harnack lecture. The detachment was fortunate. My introduction to critical historical study was not complicated by apologetic interests. One could learn objective historical research without concern as to its results. . . . I have always been thankful that my apprenticeship in historical method was not in the theological field.[11]

Egbert C. Smyth, leader of the Andover theology which had an important liberalizing influence on American religious thought early in the period under study,[12] was at the universities of Halle and Berlin in 1862–1863. " Both expounding and following Schleiermacher," Smyth later held that certainty is immediately given in religious experience,[13] and in his Christology he was similarly indebted to the German theologian, as John Wright Buckham has shown. Smyth " knew how significant and vitalizing was the reaffirmation of the Christocentric position by Schleiermacher and later by Dorner and others, and how essential it is to maintain and advance this position." [14]

Not all the American liberals studied in Germany. Some, like William Newton Clarke, found their theological ideas taking shape under German influence at a distance. Clarke's emphasis on intuitive knowledge and his appeal to religious experience, for example, bear strong resemblance to the work of Schleiermacher, even though Clarke's theological and autobiographical writings do not acknowledge that indebtedness.

This is by no means to say that the liberals were uncritical of German theology. To take Rauschenbusch as a single example, we have already seen that he believed Ritschl's theology to be defective for the simple reason that Ritschl " was born too early to get sociological ideas." [15] Though he knew the work of the German Biblical scholars and was aware that their cataclysmic eschatological view of the Kingdom in the teaching of Jesus was antithetical to his own, Rauschenbusch held tenaciously to the developmental view that shaped his entire theology. Smucker speculates plausibly that, had Troeltsch's work appeared somewhat earlier in his theological career, Rauschenbusch would probably have found it necessary to reject its historical relativism in view of his own confidence that objective scholarship is able to recover the historical Jesus in the Biblical record.[16]

Nevertheless, most American liberals would have agreed with Rauschenbusch in applying the honored term " prophet " to the German theologians.

> Among the earlier German theologians Friedrich Schleiermacher, Richard Rothe, and Albrecht Ritschl seem to me to deserve that title. The constructive genius of Schleiermacher worked out solidaristic conceptions of Christianity which were far ahead of his time. Ritschl built his essential ideas of the kingdom of evil and the Kingdom of God on Schleiermacher's work, and stressed the teaching of Luther that our service to God consists, not in religious performances, but in the faithful work we do in our secular calling. The practical importance of these elements of Ritschl's theology is proved by the strong social spirit pervading the younger Ritschlian school. . . . Professor Herrmann and Professor Troeltsch have definitely faced the relation between systematic theology and the social task of Christianity.[17]

In another place, Rauschenbusch wrote that " we shall not get away again from the central proposition of Harnack's History of Dogma, that the development of Catholic dogma was the process of the Hellenization of Christianity; in other words, that alien influences streamed into the religion of Jesus Christ and created a theology which he never taught nor intended." [18]

Because the German theologians were among the chief creators of the atmosphere that gave bone and breath to liberalism in America, it is to them that we turn first in examining liberalism's theological heritage.

1. *Friedrich Daniel Ernst Schleiermacher* (1768–1834) had perhaps the most lasting and profound influence, not simply

upon the liberal movement but as well upon the theologians who succeeded the liberals. Schleiermacher's systematic exposition of Christian doctrine, *The Christian Faith,*[19] appeared in 1821. H. R. Mackintosh has said of it:

> Next to the *Institutes* of Calvin, it is the most influential dogmatic work to which evangelical Protestantism can point, and it has helped to teach theology to more than three generations. One could no more understand present-day systematic thought without this book — its faults equally with its virtues — than one could understand modern biology without Darwin.[20]

Postliberal theologians as diverse as Karl Barth and Paul Tillich have paid tribute to Schleiermacher. Barth estimates his importance in terms scarcely less extravagant than those of Mackintosh:

> The first place in a history of the theology of the most recent times belongs and will always belong to Schleiermacher, and he has no rival. . . . What he said of Frederick the Great in his Academy address entitled, " What goes to make a great man," applies also to himself: " He did not found a school, but an era." [21]

Tillich scores neo-orthodoxy precisely because it has failed to take adequate account of Schleiermacher's theological method. " No present-day theology," says Tillich,

> should avoid a discussion of Schleiermacher's experiential method, whether in agreement or disagreement. One of the causes for the disquieting effect of neo-orthodox theology was that it detached itself completely from Schleiermacher's method, consequently denying the theological development of the last two hundred years (one hundred before and one hundred after Schleiermacher).[22]

The themes that are given systematic treatment in *The Christian Faith* were anticipated twenty years earlier in a volume of speeches on religion which Schleiermacher addressed to the " cultured despisers " of religion among his own contemporaries, and together these two books set many of the terms of the subsequent liberal argument. Schleiermacher rejected an understanding of religion defined in terms either of knowledge or of practical action. " Piety," he insisted, " cannot be an instinct craving for a mess of metaphysical and ethical crumbs." [23]

Rather, true religion is an affection, a feeling or intuition, and whoever would find true religion must examine the state of his own consciousness.

> The sum total of religion is to feel that, in its highest unity, all that moves us in feeling is one; to feel that aught single and particular is only possible by means of this unity; to feel, that is to say, that our being and living is a being and living in and through God.[24]

Religion, then, is " sense and taste for the Infinite "; [25] it is " the immediate consciousness of the universal existence of all finite things, in and through the Infinite, and of all temporal things in and through the Eternal." [26] The world is full of events which excite this intuition, for

> the Universe is ceaselessly active and at every moment is revealing itself to us. Every form it has produced, everything to which, from the fulness of its life, it has given a separate existence, every occurrence scattered from its fertile bosom is an operation of the Universe upon us. Now religion is to take up into our lives and to submit to be swayed by them, each of these influences and their consequent emotions, not by themselves but as a part of the Whole, not as limited and in opposition to other things, but as an exhibition of the Infinite in our life.[27]

The effect of this experience of primal unity is an awareness of absolute dependence upon the Ground of that unity, which is to say, absolute dependence upon God. In our relations with nature, we are aware both of acting and of being acted upon; but in our relation to nature's Ground — to God —

> neither is there . . . an immediate feeling of freedom, nor can the feeling of dependence in relation to Him be such that a feeling of freedom can be its counterpart. On the contrary, at the highest point of Christian devotion and with the clearest consciousness of the most unimpeded self-activity, the absoluteness of the feeling of dependence remains undiminished.[28]

It is precisely this feeling of absolute dependence, this sense of God's immediate certitude, which replaces the classical rational arguments for the existence of God.

The business of theology, in Schleiermacher's view, is to explicate the content of this distinctive consciousness. The Kantian influence on Schleiermacher (as a student, he fled from the philosophically circumscribed life of the Moravian seminary at Barby to Halle where he would be free to read Kant) is seen in his insistence that it is possible to speak of God only in terms of this experience in which God is turned toward us; beyond the immediacy of the religious intuition, God is both unseen and inaccessible. Reflection on the experience itself, however, permits us to assert the goodness of creation, both of the world and of man within the world. By this Schleiermacher meant that the world is so created and constructed that it is filled with stimuli which give rise to the distinctive religious experience, and that man, once he gives himself to that experience, finds a medium which is increasingly responsive. Nevertheless, Schleiermacher recognized the reality of sin. Sin arises out of a conflict between the " flesh," the lower powers of man's nature, and the God-consciousness, the former generating resistance against the latter. Sin is, therefore, to be seen as a vaunted self-sufficiency that rejects the legitimate claim of absolute dependence given in the God-consciousness.

But since " Christian piety traces everything at all connected with the God-consciousness either to sin or to grace," [29] sin requires to be defined and discussed only in the context of redemption. Indeed,

> since in our statements about sin we are to keep in view those still to be made about grace, we may regard sin on the one hand as simply that which would not be unless redemption was to be; or on the other as that which, as it is to disappear, can disappear only through redemption.[30]

Though the sufficient cause of sin is to be found in the human will, men do not will their redemption:

> Whatever alienation from God there is in the phases of our experience, we are conscious of it as an action originating in ourselves, which we call Sin; but whatever fellowship with God there is, we are conscious of it as resting upon a communication from the Redeemer, which we call Grace.[31]

The power of redemption in Jesus Christ lies in " the constant potency of His God-consciousness, which was a veritable existence of God in Him." [32] Christ's work of redemption is to induce in men an approach to his own perfect God-consciousness, and this he does by calling men into fellowship and association with him. When this happens, a new creation appears, namely, the church. Whereas association with Christ provides the inner change in man's condition, the appearance of the church provides the change in the world, since it provides a structure and fellowship of those who are attentive to the God-consciousness, within which the religious experience of the individual finds support and stimulus. The essential difference between Protestant and Roman forms of Christianity, said Schleiermacher, is that in Protestantism our relation to the church depends upon our relation to Christ, while in Romanism our relation to Christ depends upon our relation to the church.[33]

The absolute centrality of Christ in Schleiermacher's theological system is seen in his famous definition of Christianity as

> a monotheistic faith, belonging to the teleological [that is to say, ethical] type of religion . . . essentially distinguished from other such faiths by the fact that in it everything is related to the redemption accomplished by Jesus of Nazareth.[34]

Out of this brief summary of Schleiermacher's position emerge several influences that gave character to the liberal movement. (*a*) Confidence in truth discerned by intuition — the self-evident character of truth about the divine and human natures — can be traced in the failure of the later liberals to develop an explicit theological doctrine of inspiration. One is convicted of the truth of Scripture simply by submitting himself to its self-authenticating witness. (*b*) The appeal to experience, and the insistence that data for theology emerge from an examination of the state of self-consciousness rather than from Bible or creed, strengthened the claim of liberalism to be an experiential religion rather than a religion of speculation. (*c*) Emphasis on the immediate state of consciousness helps to account for the lack of historical interest among many of the liberals. (*d*) The origins of a new psychology of religion can be seen taking shape in Schleiermacher's work, and this presaged the importance which the social sciences generally were to have in the later liberalism. (*e*) The religious education movement gained impetus from Schleiermacher's idea of the nurturing of the God-consciousness in the Christian fellowship. (*f*) Although Schleiermacher does not quite come out with a moral influence theory of Christ's redemptive work, he is not far from it; and that, certainly, was the most widespread explanation of the atonement employed by the liberals. (*g*) Schleiermacher's explicit Christocentrism helped to shape the liberals' view of the person and work of Christ.

2. While Schleiermacher's theological system was built about a single focus — the experience of the God-consciousness — thus rejecting the primary significance of knowledge and practical action for faith, the theological system of *Albrecht Ritschl* (1822–1889) raised the ethical to a position of coimportance with the religious. The Christian faith, in Ritschl's view, is an ellipse having two foci — one is the redemption which is wrought in Christ, and the other is the Kingdom of God. The inseparability of these two is seen in the fact that " Christ made the universal moral Kingdom of God His end, and thus He came to know and decide for that kind of redemption which He achieved through the maintenance of fidelity in His calling. . . ." [35] The Kingdom of God is here understood as " the moral organization of humanity through love-prompted action." [36] The redemption, which Christian faith offers, consists of justification — the forgiveness of sins and the removal of guilt which creates moral separation from God — and of reconciliation, whereby man's mistrust of God is replaced by a willing assent to God's purposes.[37] Thus, Ritschl entitled his major theological work *The Christian Doctrine of Justification and Reconciliation.*

With the deliberate aim of correcting what he considered the one-sidedness of Schleiermacher, Ritschl defined Christianity as

the monotheistic, completely spiritual, and ethical religion, which, based on the life of its Author as Redeemer and as Founder of the

Kingdom of God, consists in the freedom of the Children of God, involves the impulse to conduct from the motive of love, aims at the moral organization of mankind, and grounds blessedness on the relation of sonship to God, as well as on the Kingdom of God.[38]

Sin, as Ritschl viewed it, is the opposite of reverence and trust toward God. It results from " an unrestrained repetition of selfish resolves " which generate " an ungodly and selfish bias." [39] Sin is not to be attributed to the fully conscious and willful opposition of man to the purposes of God; rather, it is confirmed in man's behavior by his ignorance of the good. Men are like children who act on the ignorant assumption that they have unlimited control over the objects and circumstances of their environment. There is, indeed, no a priori reason that the sinless life is not, in principle, possible, since we only arrive at a conviction concerning the universality of sin " by reckoning up the sum total of experiences." [40] Nevertheless, Ritschl affirmed that sin " as a mode of action and as a habitual propensity extends over the whole human race. . . ." [41] In fact, sin " unites all men with one another by means of the countless interrelations of sinful conduct " in a kingdom of sin, which is the opposite of the Kingdom of God.[42]

The uniqueness of Christ lies in the fact that his lifework was the work of God, which is to say that

the personal self-end of Christ has the same content as is contained in the self-end of God, which content Christ knew and adopted as such, in accordance with the fact that He was already known and loved by God Himself as the Bearer of the Divine self-end.[43]

The redemptive power of Christ lies in his ability to overcome sin and to reproduce his own faithful life in the lives of those who join his company, and this redemptive power is precisely what Ritschl meant when he spoke of the divinity of Christ. Jesus Christ has done for us what only God could do, Ritschl said in effect, and therefore Christ has the value of God for us. The Lordship of Christ is not a formal principle but " must be demonstrated to us in Christ's influence upon ourselves." [44]

But if Christ by what He has done and suffered for my salvation is my Lord, and if, by trusting for my salvation to the power of what He has done for me, I honour Him as my God, then that is a value-judgment of a direct kind. It is not a judgment which belongs to the sphere of disinterested scientific knowledge, like the formula of Chalcedon. . . . The nature of God and the Divine we can only know in its essence by determining its value for our salvation. . . . [We must] understand the Godhead of Christ, if it is to be understood at all, as an attribute revealed to us in His saving influence upon ourselves.[45]

Indeed, Ritschl found it difficult to know in what other way it would be possible to speak of God than in terms of his direct influence upon us, since, except for this, God's being is hidden from us. It is not even possible to entertain the question, *how* Christ could be what he is, since that question transcends all inquiry and thus is not an appropriate subject for theology.[46]

Redemption in Christ is not effected mystically and individually, but historically and communally. Since the influence of Christ finds its norm in his historical person, " therefore the Godhead or universal lordship of Christ must be apprehended in definite features of His historical life, as an attribute of His existence in time." [47] The believer must be able to experience Christ in his own history, must be able to reach Christ in his own environment; but it is only in the community of those who are devoted to Christ that Christ can become the historical environment for the believer. Therefore, for Ritschl it is impossible for anyone properly to assess the significance of Christ and thus to participate in his redemption apart from the church.

Justification, or reconciliation, as positively connected with the historical manifestation and activity of Christ, is related in the first instance to the whole of the religious community founded by Christ, which maintains the Gospel of God's grace in Christ as the direct means of its existence, and to individuals only as they attach themselves, by faith in the Gospel, to this community.[48]

Authentic and complete knowledge of Jesus' religious significance . . . depends, then, on one's reckoning oneself part of the community which He founded. . . .[49]

The crucial importance of the church does not, however, compromise Christ's essential mediatorial role; rather

> the community both is the medium for our clear remembrance of Christ, and, in spite of all defects of knowledge and of religious and moral practice, exerts an impulse to the religious estimate of self which corresponds to the specific action of Christ.[50]

Two major currents within the American liberal movement correspond to the contrasting views of Schleiermacher and Ritschl. Although Schleiermacher made a place for the church in his theology, its role is distinctly secondary to the experience of the God-consciousness. Indeed, it is easy to see that his emphasis upon individual experience could encourage those who would later appropriate his thought to ignore its communal element in the interest of the individual. Not so in the case of Ritschl, however, since in his view the church is the indispensable primary locus of God's historically rooted redemption.

A second and closely related issue concerns the apparent lack of historical interest in Schleiermacher and the veritable historicism of Ritschl. Indeed, Ritschl specifically criticized Schleiermacher because the latter gave insufficient attention to the history of religion. This was seen most vividly in Schleiermacher's almost total disinterest in the Old Testament, believing it to be irrelevant to the understanding of the New, while Ritschl, on the other hand, viewed the Old Testament as "the stage prefatory to Christianity" with "characteristics analogous to those of Christianity itself."[51]

Perhaps these divergences between the two men help to account for the subsequent contrasts between two of the chief figures of the American liberal movement, William Newton Clarke and William Adams Brown. At many points these two were in such complete agreement that Brown was able virtually to take over into his own system most of the insights of Clarke. Brown found it necessary to construct his own system, however, because of what he considered two critical omissions from Clarke's work — its almost total lack of historical material and the complete omission of any explicit treatment of the doctrine of the church.

Other Ritschlian influences on the later liberalism are these: (*a*) The rejection of metaphysics as a legitimate theological enterprise and the preference for the experiential and experimental over the speculative, while found in Schleiermacher, received even more energetic and forceful statement in Ritschl. (*b*) The historicism, which was to be a mark of the liberal movement, and the importance attached to the recovery of the historical Jesus, as well as the confidence in the reliability of that historical recovery, are complements to its antimetaphysical bias. (*c*) The centrality Ritschl gave to the Kingdom of God, his definition of the Kingdom in terms of the moral organization of the human community according to the will of God, and his correlative view of that social solidarism which spawns the kingdom of evil were widely adopted and are seen with special clarity in the work of Walter Rauschenbusch. (*d*) Ritschl's understanding of sin as the product of selfishness and ignorance gave the liberals one of their most frequently used definitions.

3. Three other German theologians, though of lesser stature than Schleiermacher or Ritschl, are, nevertheless, important to an understanding of American liberalism.

Wilhelm Herrmann (1846–1922), who was Karl Barth's theological mentor, was also one of the chief channels by which the German influence was mediated to American liberal thought. In his major work, *The Communion of the Christian with God,*[52] Herrmann insisted that no amount of induction from generalized human experience will yield communion with God. God can only come to meet us in history; he is hidden from us in nature because we do not find our whole selves there. Only as we become aware of our historical environment are we led into the presence of those facts which can reveal God to us.

> Hence the Christian religion is inseparable from those moral activities in which we become conscious of personal fellowship and its laws, and take our part in the same. It is only when we share these

moral activities that we first begin to live in that world in which we can become aware of God.[53]

God makes himself known to us through a fact, on the strength of which we can believe in him. There is only one fact that gives us this confidence, the appearance of Jesus in history.

Our certainty of God has its roots in the fact that within the realm of history to which we ourselves belong, we encounter the man Jesus as an undoubted reality. Inasmuch as Jesus raises us into fellowship with God, He is to us the Christ.[54]

In spite of the difficulties that Biblical scholarship puts in the way of historical certainty, some details of the New Testament record can be established with confidence: The fact that Jesus lived we learn from the fact of the existence of his church and its historical significance, and this in turn confirms certain aspects of the portrait of Jesus in the New Testament. But historical judgment, even when it approaches certainty, is not sufficient to create faith. What the New Testament offers is not simply the external events of Jesus' history, it also

discloses . . . the power and personality of Jesus, for that personality never lets the contradictions and imperfections of the story disfigure the clear features of that which it gave to men, namely, Jesus' own inner life.[55]

Only as one is drawn into the inner life of Jesus does genuine reconciliation with God become possible.

We . . . become conscious of God's communion with us by the fact that the Person of Jesus reveals itself to us through the power of His inner life. On this fact alone is based the peculiarity of the Christian religion.[56]

Herrmann, like Ritschl before him, vigorously rejected the mystic way of communion with God. The mystic seeks God in his own inner life, leaving Christ behind.

We cannot enter into the same relation to God which Jesus had; that remains his own secret. But we never enter upon the relation to God into which the redemption of Christ brings us, if when we find God, we lose Jesus.[57]

How, then, does one find access to the inner life of Jesus? We are drawn into that life when we join the community of his faithful. Jesus' inner life was first experienced by the primitive community of the disciples, and it is the continuing community of faithful discipleship which has preserved and transmitted his emancipating influence. We in turn come to that experience of emancipation only when we meet men on whom it has worked its effect. " Thus we never apprehend the most important element in the historical appearance of Jesus until His people make us feel it." [58]

One who is drawn into the inner life of Jesus finds the content of Jesus' own spiritual experience — his assurance of victory, of the rightness of his cause, of his moral sinlessness. Discovering these, the believer finds that he must acknowledge Jesus Christ as the one who defines the believer's own duty and who thus becomes the standard of the believing conscience. As the believer reflects on these things, he becomes conscious of a Power that can in fact guarantee the victory of Jesus Christ, and in this experience he finds for the first time an experience of the living God. But he also becomes troubled by the fact that his apprehension of Jesus involves an awareness not only of goodness but of judgment. Still, Jesus is the friend of sinners, and since the God of Jesus has now become the God of the believer, the believer knows himself to be received and accepted by God.

So for Herrmann, the most important meaning of the confession of Christ's deity is that when we confront Jesus we have to do with the living God, because in Jesus Christ we are raised into communion with the living God.

Adolf von Harnack (1851–1930) is a source, as he is a chief example, of the confidence that characterized the liberals' use of historical and critical tools in discovering " the real religion of Jesus." Harnack sought to isolate " the essence of Christianity," which he described as simple and sublime: " it means one thing and one thing only: Eternal life in the midst of time, by the strength and under the eyes of God." [59] Similarly, Harnack undertook to reduce the teaching of Jesus to its essentials:

If . . . we take a general view of Jesus' teaching, we shall see that it may be grouped under three heads. They are each of such a nature as to contain the whole, and hence it can be exhibited in its entirety under any one of them.

Firstly, the kingdom of God and its coming.

Secondly, God the Father and the infinite value of the human soul.

Thirdly, the higher righteousness and the commandment of love.[60]

Such a formulation gave encouragement and confidence to the frequent distinction made by liberals between the religion *of* Jesus and the religion *about* Jesus. Harnack did not go as far as some of the later theologians in accusing the apostle Paul of perverting the simple religion of the Gospels by turning it into the tortured and complex theology of the Epistles.

Without doing violence to the inner and essential features of the Gospel — unconditional trust in God as the Father of Jesus Christ, confidence in the Lord, forgiveness of sins, certainty of eternal life, purity and brotherly fellowship — Paul transformed it into the universal religion, and laid the ground for the great Church.[61]

But Harnack did prepare the way for the later charges against Paulinism by his suggestion that, if Paul's own faith did not do violence to the inner and essential features of the Gospel, nevertheless " the way in which he ordered his religious conceptions, as the outcome of his speculative ideas, unmistakably exercised an influence in a wrong direction." [62]

Harnack is the source of the inclination in much of liberalism to overleap the whole of Christian history from the end of the Biblical period to the Reformation, for it was his opinion, widely adopted, that the Christian faith during that period underwent " acute Hellenization " to its own disadvantage.

The eagerness with which Harnack's theological work was received is suggested by the fact that his original lectures on the essence of Christianity, treating all of the above themes, first appeared in print in 1900, and by 1927 the volume had gone through fourteen printings and had been translated widely into other languages. Rudolf Bultmann, in his introduction to the 1957 Harper Torchbook edition of the book, notes that " at the beginning of our century it exerted an extraordinary influence not only on the rising generation of theologians but also on the educated classes generally." [63]

The views of *Ernst Troeltsch* (1865–1923), the last of the German theologians to be considered here, have been helpfully summarized by H. R. Mackintosh in the following paragraph:

All religions come within a uniform field of development, though not in a single line of evolution. The deepest thing in them all is not primitive animism, or the craving for happiness, or any kind of speculative impulse to explain the world. It is mystical and intuitive contact with the supersensible. Nor, again, is the history of religions to be regarded as but a confused medley of random or opposed tendencies. On the contrary, it exhibits a real forward movement, and makes for a goal whose nature we can elicit and describe after careful study of the facts. One religion amongst the others is Christianity. It took its rise in a syncretistic Judaism, gathering up into itself various elements from other faiths. The whole process is one to be interpreted by the same laws of advancing change as obtain elsewhere.[64]

So, as Troeltsch formulated it, the law of *criticism* holds that historical judgments never rise above the level of moral certainty. The law of *relativity* insists that history is a vast continuum of events, with each to be understood not in terms of uniqueness but in its relation to all other similarly conditioned events. The law of *analogy* claims that what appear to be distinctive tenets of one faith have their analogous counterparts in other faiths.[65]

In his early work, Troeltsch held Christianity to be the culmination of man's religious development, the convergence of the religions of law (Judaism, Islam) and the religions of redemption (Hinduism, Buddhism). In his book on *The Absolute Validity of Christianity,* written shortly after 1900, Troeltsch had held that, in spite of its relative character, Christianity is

a developing religion, constantly striving towards a fresh and fuller expression. We may content ourselves with acknowledging that it possesses the highest degree of validity attained among all the historical religions which we are able to examine. We shall not wish to become Jews, nor Zoroastrians, nor Mohammedans, nor again Confucianists or Buddhists. We shall rather strive continually to bring our Christianity into harmony with the challenging conditions of life, and to bring its human and divine potentialities to the fullest possible fruition. It is the loftiest and most spiritual revelation we know at all. It has the highest validity. Let that suffice.[66]

But twenty years later in his lecture on " The Place of Christianity Among the World Religions," Troeltsch took a somewhat different view of the matter. The historical research that resulted in his monumental *Social Teaching of the Christian Churches* had led him, he said, to a new appreciation of the character of individuality in history, where individuality means the radical relativity of events. He had thus concluded that " a religion, in the several forms assumed by it, always depends upon the intellectual, social, and national conditions among which it exists." [67] Western Christianity is thus dependent for its specific character upon the classical culture of the Latin and Germanic races; in its Eastern Orthodox or Oriental forms, Christianity takes a quite different type. Since the culture upon which the religion depends is not permanent, the religion itself may in time disappear. It is, therefore, no longer possible to speak of a forward development of religions and to establish on objective criteria the superiority of Christianity; it is only possible to confess the supreme validity of Christian faith *for us*.

But this does not preclude the possibility that other racial groups, living under entirely different cultural conditions, may experience their contact with the Divine Life in a quite different way, and may themselves also possess a religion which has grown up with them, and from which they cannot sever themselves so long as they remain what they are. And they may quite sincerely regard this as absolutely valid for them, and give expression to this absolute validity according to the demands of their own religious feeling.[68]

Thus Troeltsch, whose study of the history of religions had begun with the search for the spiritual essence which all forms of religion held in common, came finally to think that task impossible. " What was really common to mankind, and universally valid for it," he said, " seemed, in spite of a general kinship and capacity for mutual understanding, to be at bottom exceedingly little, and to belong more to the province of material goods than to the ideal values of civilization." [69] His pessimism was not, however, communicated to many liberals who had been influenced by his earlier optimism and who persisted in their insistence on the essential spiritual unity of all " high " religion.

It may also be noted that the historical relativism which had its source in Troeltsch was one of the influences that created the reaction *against* liberalism in such a later theologian as H. Richard Niebuhr.[70]

B. An English Theologian

In his survey of *Progressive Religious Thought in America,* John Wright Buckham identified the English poet, philosopher, and theologian *Samuel Taylor Coleridge* (1772–1834) as "*the* philosopher of the progressive school of theology in America." If Coleridge was not the source of idealism and intuitivism as they came to expression in American liberal thought, he was, nevertheless, in Buckham's view, " their philosophical exponent and authority." [71]

Coleridge was introduced to American readers by his most avid American disciple, John Marsh, who was president and professor of philosophy in the University of Vermont and one of the leading teachers of philosophical idealism during the first third of the nineteenth century. It is reported that the Marsh edition of Coleridge's *Aids to Reflection* [72] was for Horace Bushnell the most important influence outside of the Bible.

> Emerson, too, and the " Transcendentalists " were more indebted to Coleridge than to any other modern philosopher. An influence almost as great was exerted by the " Aids " upon a number of other of the most thoughtful of American theologians and ministers, including such contrasted minds as James Freeman Clarke and W. G. T. Shedd, and through Marsh and Bushnell Coleridge spoke to Washington Gladden and others and through them to the people. . . .[73]

The " Preliminary Essay " with which Marsh introduced the American edition of the *Aids* in 1829 makes clear those aspects of Coleridge's thought that seemed to speak with peculiar pointedness to the American situation. There was, for one thing, a strong prejudice among many American theologians against admitting philosophy to the theological enterprise. They identified philosophical rationalism as the enemy of revealed truth and philosophical speculation as the nemesis of faith. What Coleridge had attempted, said Marsh, was precisely " a philosophical statement and vindication of the distinctively spiritual and peculiar doctrines of the Christian system." [74] At his hands, philosophy was not the enemy of faith but rather gave to faith its proper primacy. Coleridge held that Christian truth is not the product of reason, but once it appears, Christian truth is seen to be in accord with reason. For a Christian to believe what is irrational or absurd is to deny his nature as a rational being; but there are not two forms of reason, one for philosophy and another for theology. Reason is single and, whether in philosophy or theology, that which contradicts reason cannot be an article either of knowledge or of faith. So far from being the antithesis of reason, " Christian faith is the perfection of reason." [75] Coleridge as a philosopher was essentially engaged in a work of theodicy, " to reconcile reason with revelation, and thus to justify the way of God to man." [76] In Marsh's view, Coleridge's work

> is to be considered a philosophical work, [in] that it proves the doctrines of the Christian Faith to be rational, and exhibits philosophical grounds for the possibility of a truly *spiritual* religion. The *reality* of those experiences, or states of being, which constitute experimental or spiritual religion, rests on other grounds. It is incumbent on the philosopher to free them from the contradictions of reason, and nothing more; and who will deny, that to do this is a purpose worthy of the ablest philosopher and the most devoted Christian? [77]

A second reason for Coleridge's strong attractiveness was that he provided a viable alternative to the reigning philosophical materialism and " necessitarianism " espoused by the followers of John Locke. Locke's philosophy, said Marsh, made it impossible to distinguish between the " natural " and the " spiritual," since both were compassed by Locke within a single system, with the same laws of cause and effect applied to moral and spiritual experience as to physical events. Coleridge declared his " direct opposition " to the notion " that motives act on the will, as bodies act on bodies; and that whether mind and matter are essentially the same, or essentially different, they are both alike under one and the same law of compulsory causation." [78] If this were true, man would be no better than the brute, whose being is determined by forces outside himself and who is thus bound to act according to the irresponsible laws of nature. Yet all moral experience — the sense of moral obligation and of remorse, for example — contradicts such a view and suggests the presence in man of a self-determining will whose very character as freedom makes man morally responsible. So Coleridge wrote:

> . . . I profess a deep conviction that man was and is a fallen creature, not by accidents of bodily constitution or any other cause . . . but as diseased in his will, in that will which is the true and only strict synonyme of the word, I, or the intelligent Self.[79]

It is clear from this that Coleridge's doctrine of man as a spiritual being — self-determined and precisely for that reason morally responsible — did not lead him to an unrelieved optimism about man's moral possibilities. The influence of Calvin was too deep in him for that. Prof. W. G. T. Shedd, who edited the American edition of Coleridge's collected works, wrote that

> although Coleridge insists earnestly and at length upon the doctrine of free self-determination, he is equally earnest and decided in affirming the absolute bondage and helplessness of the fallen human Will. According to him, the Will is capable of absolutely originating its states — its holy state only in concurrence with, and aided by, the One Holy Will which is the ground and support of all finite holiness, and in its sinful state without any aid or concurrence, on the part of the Infinite Will — but when the evil moral state has once been originated, and the Will has once responsibly formed its sinful character and nature, a central radical change in the direction and tendency of this faculty is, from the very nature of the case, then out of its power.[80]

It was precisely because the prevailing philosophy of the day was unable to take sin with radical seriousness as sin that it was also unable to appreciate the unique spiritual freedom of man which, in Coleridge's view, distinguished him from the natural orders of creation.

Third, President Marsh was persuaded that " obstacles to the influence of truth exist in the speculative and metaphysical opinions generally adopted in this century. . . ." [81] Because Coleridge held that supersensory — that is to say, spiritual — truth is apprehended by intuition rather than by the methods of induction or abstraction, he was welcomed as an ally by the embattled opponents of the American phase of the Enlightenment. Coleridge distinguished between understanding and reason. Understanding, " considered exclusively as an organ of human intelligence, is the faculty by which we reflect and generalize," he wrote.[82] The process of understanding involves three acts: " first, the appropriation of our attention; second . . . abstraction, or the voluntary withholding of attention; and, third, generalization." [83] The understanding thus deals competently only with the data of the senses and must always be referred to that data for its own verification; which is to say that the understanding requires to be submitted to faculties outside itself for its authentication. Man shares understanding with the beasts. Reason, on the other hand, " is the power of universal and necessary convictions, the source and substance of truths above sense, and having their evidence in themselves." [84] Reason " is a direct aspect of truth, an inward beholding, having a similar relation to the intelligible or spiritual, as Sense has to the material or phenomenal." [85] Dependence on the understanding leads finally to skepticism in view of the ephemeral and problematical character of sensory experience; only reason brings certitude. So in his *Confessions of an Inquiring Spirit,* Coleridge could affirm:

Friend! The truth revealed through Christ has its evidence in itself, and the proof of its divine authority in its fitness to our nature and needs; — the clearness and cogency of this proof being proportionate to the degree of self-knowledge in each individual hearer.[86]

On this ground, Coleridge declared his opposition to " bibliolatry," a term he apparently borrowed from Lessing. The Scriptures are not the Christian religion; rather, they record the history of the Christian religion. The truth of Christian faith rests in its immediate attestation to the human spirit rather than in reference to historical evidence. This does not mean, however, that the Bible is, therefore, reduced to unimportance. On the contrary, the fact of the relevance of the Biblical faith " to our nature and needs " clearly establishes the authority of the Biblical witness over our lives. " Christian teaching does not derive its truth from authority, but derives its authority from truth." [87] So Coleridge could confess:

> This I believe by my own dear experience; — that the more tranquilly an inquirer takes up the Bible as he would any other body of ancient writings, the livelier and steadier will be his impressions of its superiority to all other books, till at length all other books and all other knowledge will be valuable in his eyes in proportion as they help him to a better understanding of his Bible. Difficulty after difficulty has been overcome from the time that I began to study the Scriptures with free and unboding spirit, under the conviction that my faith in the Incarnate Word and his Gospel was secure, whatever the result might be; — the difficulties that still remain being so few and insignificant in my own estimation, that I have less personal interest in the question than many of those who will most dogmatically condemn me for presuming to make a question of it.[88]

Finally, Coleridge's preference for living religious experience over doctrine supported the growing quest in America for an experimental religion. Coleridge anticipated the skeptical questions, How can I comprehend Christian truth? and, How is it to be proved? and he had a ready reply:

> To the first question I should answer: Christianity is not a theory, or a speculation; but a life; — not a philosophy of life, but a life and a living process. To the second: *Try it.*[89]

So in his insistence on the reasonableness of faith, on the spiritual nature of reality, on faith established by intuitive certainty, and on experimentalism in religion, Samuel Taylor Coleridge strengthened some of the major themes that were to shape the later liberalism.

C. The Movement of American Protestant Thought

American liberal Protestantism, however much we may identify certain of its sources in German and British theological scholarship, stands in an ordered and discernible succession of theological development within the American scene itself. The most influential account of this development is that given by H. Richard Niebuhr in *The Kingdom of God in America.*[90] Niebuhr wrote that book in a mood of confession and under conviction that the kind of analysis which he had made in his earlier *Social Sources of Denominationalism*[91] was inadequate to the full significance of the development of American Protestantism. True as far as it went, his institutional analysis in the earlier work did not go far enough. For, Niebuhr later insisted, the religious development in America, as elsewhere, is essentially a living movement rather than the history of an institution or of a series of institutions. In this section we shall summarize Niebuhr's influential reconstruction of that movement.

A movement tends to take its direction from some motivating vision, Niebuhr thought, and this vision for the American religious development is the Kingdom of God. To be sure, the vision did not always have the same lineaments; and, though it involved some obvious oversimplifications, Niebuhr divided the history of the movement into three main phases.

The first was the Puritan phase in which the Kingdom of God was understood in terms of the Sovereignty of God. In his *Holy Commonwealth,* Richard Baxter had written, " the World is a Kingdom whereof God is the King . . . an absolute Monarchy . . . by the title of Creation. . . . God is the end as well as the beginning of the divine monarchy of the world " and " all men as men are the subjects of God's kingdom, as to Obligations and Duty, and God will not ask the consent of any man to be so obliged."[92] In the Puritan conviction, the Kingdom was not something to be built or established in the New World, nor was it an alien reality which would enter history from a wholly transcendent source. Rather, as Baxter implied, the Kingdom was the rule which God had established at the creation, and the function of men was to give witness to that Sovereignty, to be obedient to that rule, in spite and in the face of the world's obvious rebellion against it.

"The converse of dependence on God," as Niebuhr noted, "is independence of everything less than God." [93] Thus Puritan Calvinism had its practical issue, for one thing, in a Biblical constitutionalism

> in which the revelation of God recorded in the Scriptures was conceived as a double covenant which was not indeed the source of the laws that needed to be enacted for the common life or even wholly of the doctrines which were to be taught in the churches, but which was the constant check upon the vagrant desires of individuals or masses and upon the subjective inspirations of self-appointed prophets or the specious reasonings of self-confident wise men.[94]

Second, and as a corollary, Puritan Calvinism issued in a claim for the independence of the church from any — whether bishop, prince, or magistrate; whether religious institution or political institution — purporting to represent divine authority, thus maintaining the freedom of the church to be obedient to revealed truth. Its third issue took the form of the limitation of all human powers, whether in church or in state. John Cotton had written:

> Let all the world learn to give mortall men no greater power than they are content they shall use, for use it they will. . . . It is necessary . . . that all power that is on earth be limited, church-power or other. . . . It is counted a matter of danger to the state to limit prerogatives, but it is a further danger not to have them limited. . . . It is therefore fit for every man to be studious of the bounds which the Lord hath set; and for the People, in whom fundamentally all power lyes, to give as much power as God in his word gives to men.[95]

There is a sense in which Calvinism could be spoken of as "crisis theology," for man was seen to stand continually under the crisis of sovereign judgment, constantly under the Damoclean sword of predestinarian preoccupations. But as the first

Puritan generation passed and subsequent generations succeeded, the sense of immediate crisis in the relation between God and man faded. Whereas in the days of its strength Puritanism required a statement of personal Christian experience for membership in the church, the time came when the vividness of men's awareness of God was so dulled that no such statement of direct and immediate experience was possible. The Halfway Covenant became, then, a practical expedient; but the vigor of the Puritan Calvinism could no longer be asserted, and Puritanism ran off in an arid scholasticism. This, said Niebuhr, was the character of seventeenth century American theology.

The eighteenth century brought the second phase of the American religious movement in the form of Evangelicalism. Revivalistic awakenings began, quite without design, under the preaching of Theodore Freylinghuysen in New Jersey in 1726, and under Jonathan Edwards at Northampton in 1734. Though Edwards and his successors among the Consistent Calvinists exercised the greatest circumspection in the methods employed in the revival — they were opposed to the use of " means," believing that conviction of sin depended upon the divine activity and not on the manipulations of the revivalist — others were less inclined to caution. These others — such men as Timothy Dwight, Lyman Beecher, Nathaniel Taylor, and even more extremely Charles G. Finney and the " western " revivalists — saw in revivalism the answer to the dead hand of Puritanism, which had lately been upon American religion, and they determined to exploit it to the full.

Evangelicalism understood the Kingdom of God, as Niebuhr put it, not in the " sovereignty " terms of the Puritans, but rather in terms of the Reign of Christ. This involved the proclamation that love, as found in Christ, is to replace the fear that was attendant upon an austere Puritanism. It was the announcement of a new freedom to replace the regimentation of a disciplined Puritanism. So there was agreement among the revivalists that

the kingdom of God is not a reign of terror but one of love, not of law but of liberty. God has willed to reconcile men to his will, to write his law upon their hearts, and he has done this by means of Jesus Christ. He who has become a citizen of the true kingdom of Christ, or of the invisible church, is free. He does good, he executes justice, he loves his neighbor, he has public spirit, not because he is constrained by external laws and sanctions, but because he is no longer concerned about himself and can love goodness for its own sake.[96]

So radical a change in man, from bondage to freedom, could only be effected by the God who is himself sovereign over all powers. Thus, as Niebuhr showed, the evangelical proclamation of the Reign of Christ is firmly founded in the earlier declaration of the Sovereignty of God.

Several consequences can be assigned to this period of Awakening. First, the principle of voluntaryism came to be established as the distinctive form of the religious life, whether personal or institutional. Only the voluntary yielding of one's life to God, under the personal experience of conviction of sin, could suffice for salvation; and only the voluntary association of the converted, banded together for the accomplishment of their common Christian mission to bring all men under the reign of Christ's love, could suffice for the effective evangelization of a growing nation. Second, emphasis upon personal conversion experience led to a religion of inwardness. Concern for the inner life brought about a withdrawal of Christian concern for and involvement in political affairs and its replacement with a motivation to perform acts, and to create institutions, of a charitable nature. Third, in spite of the revivalist emphasis upon personal religious experience, revival also brought renewed emphasis upon the importance of the Scriptures to the Christian life. " Scripture without experience is empty, but experience without Scripture is blind." Thus Niebuhr characterized the commonly accepted view.[97] Finally, Niebuhr showed that, although the theme of Evangelicalism was the love of God in man as revealed in Jesus Christ, the Evangelicals never made the mistake of identifying love with " amiable sentiment," or of assuming that Christian love was simply a natural affection which could be practiced apart from the converting power of God, or yet that love of neighbor was the whole of the Christian life.[98] Positively, out of the Awakening came " that sacramental sense of all existence which we miscall humanitarianism, since it was extended to more than human beings and since its basis was not the goodness of man but the goodness of God." [99]

Evangelicalism lost its fire when the organizations that it had developed for purposes of evangelization became denominations which, before long, turned into defensive institutions. Whereas in its earlier phase revivalism had seen the formation of a large number of ecumenical agencies, joint instruments of mission, with the institutional entrenchment that accompanied denominational development, that sense of catholic concern was largely lost. The reassertion of the crisis between man and God, which was in the revivalist's call, ended in the almost complete accommodation to culture as denominationalism became virtually synonymous with Americanism.

The third phase of American religious development came in the nineteenth century social gospel reaction to the demise of the revivalist spirit, and although it carries us slightly ahead of our story, we shall nevertheless deal in even more summary fashion with this third period in order to give a complete account of Niebuhr's framework for understanding the American religious tradition.

The social gospel understood the Kingdom of God in terms of a coming earthly kingdom, whose signs were to be seen on every hand:

> The hope of the coming kingdom was closely bound up with the evangelistic and humanitarian enterprises which grew and blossomed in connection with the revival movement. To many of the men who participated in them or observed them these were evidences of its coming and at the same time instruments whereby the kingdom was being hastened. The missionary movement seemed even to the most restrained among its interpreters the sign that God was preparing a great revolution.[100]

It was, indeed, a revolutionary passion that moved the men of the social gospel. Religion at their hands became thoroughly ethicized. Against the religion of inwardness and charity of the revivalists, and against the institutional accommodations to culture, the social gospel posed a challenge to accepted practices in business and industry especially, and called for sweeping social reforms in all areas of public life. Against the " gospel of wealth " of Andrew Carnegie and his fellow industrialists, the social gospel developed a searching critique of wealth and of the industrial and economic system which spawned it, and advocated instead the translation of human brotherhood into a form of Christian socialism.

In the light of the erosion of vital religion which accompanied the end of the period of revival, many men who might otherwise have renounced their faith out of disappointment or disillusionment were saved for the Christian movement by the social gospel, remaining within the circle of faith " for the work's sake."

Liberalism and its social gospel were, in the beginning, outgrowths of Evangelicalism, and Niebuhr noted that Washington Gladden and Walter Rauschenbusch

> distinguished themselves from their liberal contemporaries by keeping relatively close to evangelical notions of the sovereignty of God, of the reign of Christ and of the coming kingdom. In Rauschenbusch especially the revolutionary element remained pronounced; the reign of Christ required conversion and the coming kingdom was crisis, judgment as well as promise.[101]

But increasingly, liberalism drew apart from its Evangelical heritage and lost

> the sense of the broken relation between God and man, between the present and the coming kingdom. In the course of succeeding generations the heritage of faith with which liberalism had started was used up.[102]

The theology of the coming Kingdom, with its note of crisis and judgment, became the optimistic secular doctrine of progress strengthened by the new confidence in biological evolution and its translation into social Darwinism. Finally, institutional conservatism overtook the liberal movement, and the reformers came to seem

less interested in the worker than in winning him to the church, that is, of using the social gospel as a means for the maintenance of the institution. As reformers they turned, when persuasion failed, to political means, in order that good social habits of temperance and Sabbath observance might be maintained. As propagandists they sought the extension of democratic institutions — if necessary by recourse to military force — in order that all the world might share in the blessings of the kingdom of God on earth.[103]

So, Niebuhr concluded, " in institutional liberalism as in institutional Evangelicalism and Protestantism the aggressive movement of the kingdom of God in America had apparently come to a stop." [104]

Thus, liberalism found its place in three centuries of American religious experience.

D. Two American Forerunners of Liberalism

Two important figures — *Nathaniel William Taylor* (1786–1858) and *Horace Bushnell* (1802–1876) — bridge the transition from the inherited orthodoxy of the eighteenth century to the liberalism of the nineteenth century.[105] Neither Taylor nor Bushnell can be denominated a liberal in the terms of the present study. Taylor died the year before Darwin's *Origin of Species* appeared. Bushnell was well acquainted with the Darwinian view, but he rejected its specific theory of the transmutation of species,[106] and in *Nature and the Supernatural,* written in 1850, he inveighed against the pre-Darwinian notion of developmentalism and its concomitant naturalistic world view.[107] Nevertheless, Taylor and Bushnell are significant both because of the theological influence which each exercised in his own right, and because each anticipated certain theological themes, largely absent from American orthodoxy, which were to find fuller expression in the liberal movement.

During the Puritan period, the " federal " doctrine of original sin was virtually unquestioned among orthodox Calvinists. Promulgated in the Westminster Confession and in the Larger and Shorter Catechisms, this doctrine held that man's first parents " fell from their original righteousness," thus becoming " wholly defiled in all the faculties and parts of soul and body." [108] Since Adam and Eve were " the root of all mankind, the guilt of this sin was imputed, and the same death in sin and corrupted nature conveyed to all their posterity, descending from them by ordinary generation." [109] What made this doctrine " federal " was the further view that Adam was a " public person," [110] literally a representative man, in whom all his progeny were representatively present and for whom all his progeny thus bear responsibility. As all mankind was represented in the Fall, so also had all mankind been represented in the covenant which God made with Adam, " not for himself only, but for his posterity." [111] Thus, as H. Shelton Smith has noted, the Puritans held a " double grip " on the doctrine of original sin, since " the first idea predicates a direct participation, and the second a representative participation in Adam's first sin." [112]

This doctrine remained essentially unchanged until the latter half of the eighteenth century when it faced challenges from two directions. One challenge came initially from those who had been influenced by the English Enlightenment, such as Daniel Whitby and John Taylor.[113] It came to full flower in the Unitarian protest after the turn of the century, especially under the leadership of William Ellery Channing, Theodore Parker, and Ralph Waldo Emerson. The Unitarians charged that the Calvinistic notion of man's innate and total depravity is empirically insupportable. Smith has summarized the argument of Unitarian Henry Ware, Hollis Professor of Divinity at Harvard, as follows:

(1) If it be true that children exhibit sinful affections, it is also true that they manifest good affections. (2) If depraved affections exhibit themselves very early, so do good affections. (3) If sinful affections cannot be traced to any radical change produced in the child's natural constitution subsequent to birth, neither can virtuous affections. (4) If sinful reactions are spontaneous and not easily eradicable, so are virtuous reactions. (5) If it is predictable that all chil-

dren will certainly sin, it is no less predictable that they will also certainly manifest some good traits.[114]

Why, the Unitarians asked, should one set of data carry greater moral significance than the other? Furthermore, even if the innate depravity of man could be established on empirical grounds, it would surely imply an unjust and immoral God. Men can be held responsible only for that over which they exercise their freedom of choice; but if their choices are determined at their creation, moral culpability for sin belongs to God and not to men. So Channing wrote, " Other errors we can pass over with comparative indifference, but we ask our opponents to leave us a God, worthy of our love and trust." [115]

A second challenge came from those who desired to maintain their connection with the Calvinist tradition but who nevertheless saw the need to reformulate the " federal " doctrine in terms which would take seriously the objections of the Unitarians. The most effective reformulation came in the so-called New Haven Theology,[116] which was developed by a number of distinguished figures, among them Lyman Beecher. The chief architect of the New Haven Theology, however, was Nathaniel William Taylor.

Taylor, who graduated from Yale College and later studied theology with President Timothy Dwight of Yale, was pastor of the First Congregational Church of New Haven from 1812 to 1822 and then became Dwight Professor of Didactic Theology at Yale, which chair he held until his death in 1858. In Taylor's theological work, it is possible to discover some of the elements that later appeared in a fully formed and self-conscious liberalism.[117]

Taylor developed his doctrine of man and sin in terms of man's free moral agency, a point on which he held that Jonathan Edwards and the later Edwardians — die-hard defenders of the " federal " doctrine — were chiefly deficient.[118] When Taylor finished his work, as Sidney Mead has commented, it could be seen simply as a more sophisticated explication of the revivalist invitation, " whosoever will may come." [119]

Sin, said Taylor, presupposes man's free moral agency, since there is no culpability without moral freedom. Prior to the first act of moral agency on the part of an individual, there is nothing in the life of that individual which can be called sin. But, Taylor added, it is true that a man will sin as soon as he is able. There is no need, however, to seek the source of that sin in some primal historical event or in a doctrine of physicalism. The human will is itself the sufficient explanation of sin. Sin is to be found in concrete actions and choices, in wrong preferences and evil acts. Taylor rejected the idea that man's moral nature is defiled and obliterated. Rather, his moral nature consists in his understanding, his will, and his conscience. If these were lost, man would cease to be human.[120]

Unlike the Unitarians, Taylor was willing to give a large place to the fact of sin and its universality, but unlike the Edwardians, he was unwilling to erect a logical structure of a speculative sort to account for it. Sin is real; a man sins as soon as he is able, and the freedom of the human will must be accepted as its own sufficient explanation.

Taylor did not feel compelled to give up totally the Calvinistic doctrine of predestination in order to make way for the doctrine of free moral agency. He attempted to maintain both by the principle of " certainty with power to the contrary ":

> There are . . . antecedents to an event which make its happening certain, but, looking back (and that is the only way one can look at his experience), one is sure that at any point in the past he had full power to choose otherwise than he did choose. . . . They always had, in other words, full power to the contrary, even though God knew in advance what they would do.[121]

The freedom of the will, in Taylor's view, extends to salvation as well as to damnation. God does not require of man more than man is able to perform. " I must " implies " I can." Indeed, man must make himself a new heart. Taylor believed that, in principle, it is possible for man to meet the requirements God sets for salvation, and if man's faith and good works do not compel God to save him, at least God gives us reason to believe that the one will follow upon the other. Thus far was Taylor prepared to compromise the Calvinist doctrine of God's absolute sovereignty.[122]

God " demands only a rational faith of rational beings," and this means that the Scriptures themselves " shall be tried at the bar of human reason." [123] But Taylor was confident that there would be no final conflict between reason and revelation. There are fixed and eternal truths that the human mind is capable of discerning; but more, once these truths are made clear, reason will give its consent. Mead suggests that this was probably the source in Taylor of what some of his contemporaries described as " arrogance," for he was sure that by independent investigation his students would come to his point of view, since that point of view embodied precisely those eternal truths about God and man to which all reasonable men must finally assent.[124]

Taylor's position, then, represents what came to be called " progressive orthodoxy," maintaining certain ties with the older Calvinism while undertaking a radical reorientation of its theological drift. Taylor's doctrine of man's free moral agency and his insistence on the capacity of man to accomplish what God requires; his willingness to compromise the sovereignty of God, limiting God's power by the degree of man's freedom; his confidence in the self-evident character of truth; his test of rational intelligibility of truth and his insistence that the Bible stand under that test — all mark him as kin to the later liberal movement.

It was in the reinterpretation of traditional views of man and sin that Horace Bushnell also made an influential and lasting contribution to the liberalizing of American theology. Bushnell, who had studied law and practiced journalism before entering Yale Divinity School in 1831, became pastor of the North Congregational Church of Hartford, Connecticut, in 1833, retiring prematurely in 1859 because of ill-health.

Man, in Bushnell's view, is the juncture of the natural and the supernatural. Man is indeed a natural being, in that he is subject to many of the necessities of natural law; but man is also a supernatural being, in the sense that he is able to act upon the chain of cause and effect relations that define the realm of nature, and to act upon that chain precisely from outside of it. In spite of the limitations that nature presses upon him, man is thus superior to the mindless world about him. Man is a power, not a thing — a power being that " agent or force which acts from itself, uncaused, initiating trains of effect that flow from itself." [125] Because man transcends the nexus of cause and effect, he is " able to act on the lines and vary the combinations of natural causalities," [126] thus making nature the servant of his own supernatural purposes and creating out of nature what nature alone could never produce.

Nature, in short, is only stage, field, medium, vehicle, for the universe; that is, for God and his powers [viz., all free intelligences]. These are the real magnitudes, because they contain, at once, the import and the final causes, or last ends, of all created substance. The grand, universal, invisible system of God, therefore, is a system that centralizes itself in these, subordinating all mere things, and having them for its instruments.[127]

Bushnell resisted stoutly the notion that living forms have emerged developmentally over long centuries out of inorganic forms. " There neither is nor can be any middle position between humanity and no humanity." [128] Living forms, rather, " are fresh creations, by a power out of nature and above it acting on nature." [129] In spite of this exalted view of human personality, Bushnell held that man is born in a " condition privative," that is, in a state of deprivation. His empirical knowledge is limited, and his moral sense and experience are limited. In view of these limitations, it is scarcely surprising that sin arises in universal fashion. Furthermore, Bushnell seems to have anticipated later developments in psychosomatic medicine, for he insisted that the disorder of the soul has an inevitable effect in the disordering of the body. Sin, therefore, has its seat in the spiritual nature of man, but it also has inescapable physical consequences.

Since Bushnell was persuaded that there is an organic solidarity which binds all mankind in a living web of influence, he was able to account for the inheritance of sin, partly in terms of the spiritual inheritance by one generation of the spiritual disorders of earlier generations, and partly by the inheritance of one generation of the physical consequences of the previous generations' sin. But if sin has this kind of organic effect, so does goodness; and if sin has its effect upon the physical organism, so does virtue. Therefore, man is the inheritor, not simply of a single stream of moral influence, but of a double stream. Thus it was possible for Bushnell to express his faith in the efficacy of Christian nurture [130] because of his confidence in the capacity of the human being to respond to moral influence and example.

It is just here that Bushnell's view of the work of Christ for man's redemption comes to focus. Moral renovation in man requires more than an objective, externalized example; it requires a subjective event. No mere model to be copied will suffice, since "something is wanted that shall go before and beget, in us, the disposition to copy an example." [131] It must also be a supernatural event.

> This, in fact, is the grand, all-conditioning truth of Christianity itself; viz., that man has no ability, in himself and merely acting by himself, to become right and perfect; and that, hence, without some extension to him from without and above, some approach and ministration that is supernatural, he can never become what his own ideals require.[132]

It is precisely this that Christ accomplishes in his threefold work on our behalf. First, by his compassionate concern for us and his suffering identification with us,

> we are softened and drawn by him, and even begin to want him entered more deeply, that we may feel him more constrainingly. In this way a great point is turned in our recovery. Our heart is engaged before it is broken. We like the Friend before we love the Saviour.[133]

Second, when we look upon the suffering of Christ, knowing that he suffers innocently on our account and that it is therefore we who have pierced him, we are pierced ourselves with a conviction of sin deeper than mere remorse. Finally, Christ offers himself, in our dereliction, as a friend, whom we can feel as a man, and whom it will be sufficiently accurate for us to accept and love. Let him come so nigh, if possible, let him be so deeply inserted into our lot and our feeling, that we can bury ourselves in him and the fortunes of his burdened life, and then it will be wonderful, if having God's own type in his life, we do not catch the true impress from it in ourselves.[134]

Thus for Bushnell, Christ is truly the Moral Power of God.

We shall look briefly at one final contribution made by Bushnell to liberalism, a contribution made by the catholicity of his temper. Bushnell lived in a period of theological controversy and he sought to find a constructive approach to that controversy that would serve the truth while respecting the integrity of the ways in which men differ. He rejected what he called the " neutral " school, the fence-sitters " who dread nothing with so great reason as combustion of any sort " and who, therefore, attempt " to divide distances and settle themselves down as nearly midway between the poles as possible." Neutrality, he held, is more sickening than controversy. He similarly rejected the " liberal " who has no creed " save that other men shall be welcome to theirs," thus making a virtue of negation and freezing " itself in the mild and gentle temperature it has mistaken for charity." Bushnell's own approach he called " comprehensive," describing it in the following terms:

In the comprehensive school it will be a first conviction that all serious and earnest men have something in their view which makes it truth to them; therefore that all serious earnest men, however repugnant in their words, have yet some radical agreement, and if the place can be found, will somewhere reveal their brotherhood. Therefore they are not only to tolerate but to love and respect each other. Nay they are each to ask, what has the other which is necessary to its own completeness in the truth? . . . The endeavor to comprehend all antagonisms and hold the just equilibrium of truth is the highest and most ingenuous that a human soul can propose; one that only God can perfectly realize.[135]

Although Bushnell did not find the term " liberal " to his liking, in this comprehensive position he came to embody that ability to take another man's view seriously without abandoning one's own, which has always characterized the liberal mind at its best.

The affinity of Bushnell with the later liberals can thus be marked at a number of points: his notion of the interaction rather than the disjunction of nature and the supernatural; the primacy he assigned to spiritual reality and especially to personality; his rejection of innate depravity and his assertion of the organic character of all human relations; his emphasis on redemption rather than social change; his explicit Christocentrism; and his catholic temper.

Having examined liberalism's theological heritage, we turn next to a detailed examination of the liberal movement itself.

Three A PROFILE OF AMERICAN THEOLOGICAL LIBERALISM 1879–1917

LIBERALISM IN late nineteenth century America represented the convergence of two vital movements.

One of these movements was Evangelicalism. The liberals were not only the successors to the period of Protestant revival, they were also its children. H. Richard Niebuhr has shown the kinship between Evangelicalism and liberalism in their sense of the sacramental character of the world because of the relation all things bear to their common Creator, in their devotion to human brotherhood under God's Fatherhood, in their earnest desire for man's internal renovation as opposed to merely external changes in behavior, in their passion for liberty, and in an optimism rooted in a profound faith in God as the Lord of history.[1] "Though liberalism often sought to deny its kinship to the historic gospel," Niebuhr concludes, "its speech and its features betrayed it."[2]

The second movement was the rising tide of secular, scientific, intellectual, and social reform. Indeed, an alliance between evangelical Christianity and secular ferment is precisely what distinguishes liberalism, in the view of some scholars. So Daniel Day Williams has written:

> By "liberal theology" I mean the movement in modern Protestantism which during the nineteenth century tried to bring Christian thought into organic unity with the evolutionary world view, the movements for social reconstruction, and the expectations of "a better world" which dominated the general mind.[3]

The degree to which the liberals succeeded in creating such an " organic unity " between the historic Christian faith and the nineteenth century world view can be judged by the following profile of liberalism in the period 1879–1917, in which the two elements are almost inextricably intermingled. Every effort is made, in filling in the profile, to allow the liberals to speak for themselves.

A. The world view of the liberal was shaped by the theory of evolution, with its view of the continuity of all life.

The acceptance of the evolved status of man was one of the chief marks of liberalism. William Newton Clarke wrote, quite unequivocally, that " if theology remands the question of the origin of the human race to anthropology and its kindred sciences, it will receive from them an evolutionary answer." [4] Clarke's own attitude toward that answer was clear: " There is no ground whatever for foes to hope or friends to fear that Christianity must retire if the evolutionary idea gains entrance." [5]

It was customary for the liberals to insist that the chief significance of evolution is to be seen not primarily in origins but in ends. So, although it was true that the theory of evolution related man to the subhuman, the whole process was viewed not so much in terms of descent but of ascent. Thus, Newell Dwight Hillis wrote that,

> as the embryo life develops it passes into and through the likeness of each lower animal, and ever journeying upward carries with it the special grace and gift of each creature it has left behind . . . until the excellencies of many lower forms are compacted in the one higher man.[6]

So, Hillis exulted,

> man's descent from the animals has been displaced by the ascent of the human body. This is not degradation, but an unspeakable exaltation. Man is " fearfully and wonderfully made." God ordained the long upward march for making his body exquisitely sensitive and fitted to be the home of a divine mind. How marvelously does this view enhance the dignity of man, and clothe God with majesty and glory.[7]

Similarly, Henry Ward Beecher could declare:

I am a cordial Christian evolutionist. . . . Man . . . is made to start and not to stop; to go on, and on, and up, and onward, steadily emerging from the controlling power of the physical and animal condition in which he was born and which enthrall him during his struggle upward, but ever touching higher elements of possibility, and ending in the glorious liberty of the sons of God.[8]

Still another aspect of the significance of evolution lay in the confidence that the appearance of man in the evolutionary process is evidence that that which is most characteristic of human life is deepest in the universe. This is seen in the affirmation of an ultimate and pervasive spiritual reality in the world, and that the cosmos is geared to the production of personality. So even when evolution leads us to consider origins, there is gain. " The old argument from design has collapsed before the doctrine of natural selection," as Walter Rauschenbusch pointed out. " But further thought has shown us that the element of design has only receded and is waiting for us at the beginning of all things." [9]

All of this is not to say that the liberals were uncritical of evolution. Theodore Munger expressed a reservation many shared when he wrote that the New Theology does not merge itself with natural science. It is not ready to " go over into the camp of natural science, and sit down under the manipulations of a doctrine of evolution, with its one category of matter and one invariable force." [10] But there was no need to substitute science for theology when evolution could be adapted to theological insight, and this, the liberals were convinced, was of immeasurable gain for the Christian cause.

The practical result of the idea of the continuity of life, given in the theory of evolution, was a new positive evaluation of the world, a new conviction about the goodness of creation. This was seen among some liberals in the passion for social justice and the equitable distribution of the material benefits of life, and among others in the positive valuation of wealth. In still others it was seen in a concern for the conservation of natural resources.

B. Liberals tended to modify explicit supernaturalism with a doctrine of the immanence of God.

Shailer Mathews hailed it as a characteristic of the modern world that it conceives of " God as immanent in this process rather than an extra-mundane monarch." [11] William Newton Clarke affirmed that God dwells in the universe and is active in the whole of it, though he also wanted to make it clear that God is not wholly occupied by the universe, nor does he exhaust his possibilities in the conduct of it. William Adams Brown acknowledged that the twentieth century has no monopoly of the doctrine of divine immanence, since Calvin believed it too.

> Yet none the less God seemed to Calvin infinitely remote from the multitudes of his creatures. The nearness which I have in mind is not of essence but of character. . . . I mean that there is nothing in God's nature which separates him from any child of man.[12]

The emergence of this emphasis on divine immanence is coincident with the appearance of the theory of evolution, and if the former cannot be equated with the latter (there is, after all, an immanentist strain in the Bible), there is, nevertheless, a close historical connection. That is, the liberal emphasis on divine immanence is the theistic expression of the scientific idea of continuity. It had, for liberalism, several consequences. One is the discrediting of miracle. Shailer Mathews wanted to replace the word " miracle " with " event," since the latter would be less offensive to the modern insistence that there can be no break in causal process. At the same time, Mathews desired to retain the significance of " signs " and " wonders " as the expression of the immanent divine personality in unique events. The older view of miracle, said William Adams Brown, was deficient in that it concentrated man's attention on the activity of God in the past.

> They tried to draw a hard-and-fast line between the miracles of the Bible and God's methods of self-disclosure to men of other races and other ages. They failed to recognize, or, at all events, adequately to

emphasize, the fact that God is as truly present, if in different degree and for different purposes, in our present experience as in the experience of the past.[13]

A second implication of the doctrine of divine immanence is the liberal blurring of the distinction between natural or general revelation on the one hand, and special revelation on the other.

Perhaps the most important consequence lies in a new sense of the kinship between man and God. Here Kierkegaard's "infinite qualitative distinction between the temporal and the eternal" is utterly foreign. It is only necessary to call the roll to see it. Newell Dwight Hillis: "Reason and memory in man answer to those faculties in God, as do conscience and the moral sentiments. In creative genius man alone is a sharer with God."[14] Henry Ward Beecher: "Does not Evolution point towards this explicit teaching of Jesus regarding the unity of man with God?"[15] George A. Gordon: "It is taken for granted that in a special way [God] is in the constitution of human reason, in the structure of society, in the moral articulation of being which is deeper than all conscious will, and which is the condition of the life proper to man."[16] Theodore Munger: "The inmost principle of revelation is that the mind of God reveals itself to the mind of man; and the basis of this principle is that one mind is made in the image of the other, and therefore capable of similar processes of thought and feeling."[17] William Newton Clarke: To know man is in a measure to know God, since man bears God's self-image. Self-knowledge and the study of human kind gives us understanding of those natural and moral qualities we attribute to God.[18] William Adams Brown: "There is nothing in God's nature which separates him from any child of man."[19]

A final citation from William Newton Clarke will serve to put the matter somewhat more fully and definitively:

> The distinctive mark of man is the capacity of the spirit; and in man's spiritual capacities is found the image of God. The constitution of man as a spirit is like that of God as a spirit, and that which distinguishes man from other beings is that which he shares with God. God and man are essentially alike in mental structure and

method: this both revelation and science yield. If this were not so, God could not be known to man.[20]

C. The liberals expressed their doctrine of man primarily in terms of divine sonship and free moral agency.

In the light of the foregoing discussion of divine immanence with emphasis upon the essentially like qualities of God and man, liberals tended to see man as created for divine sonship, a potential which needed only to be awakened. So William Newton Clarke could write that " man was created as a child of God, and the sonship that was established by the creative act of God could never be destroyed. . . ." [21] The filial relation is broken by sin, to be sure; but when it is restored, " It is not a gift of new faculties, or a creation of something additional in man, but an awakening of new dispositions which prepare him for fellowship with God." [22] The theme of sonship was a part of William Adams Brown's definition of Christianity: " the religion of divine sonship and human brotherhood. . . ." [23]

The other key to the liberal anthropology is to be found in the idea of free moral agency in man. This represented an explicit rejection of the traditional view of original sin as imputed guilt; but more positively, it is the recognition that the sufficient explanation for man's moral condition is to be found in his will. Said Clarke, " Free-will is essential to man, indispensable to moral action, and to rational action as well. Consciousness affirms it, and conscience would have no significance if it did not exist." [24] Some liberals translated this into a confidence that " I must " necessarily implies " I can." So Russell Conwell described man's future as a block of unwrought marble.

> You can work it into what you will. Neither heredity, nor environment, nor any obstacle superimposed by man can keep you from marching straight through to success, provided you are guided by a firm, driving determination, and have normal health and intelligence.[25]

But free moral agency was not always interpreted in such unrestricted terms. Other liberals were quite capable of recognizing limitations upon man's moral possibilities. They saw the significant struggle that attends man's moral maturity — struggle through personal and corporate sin as well as through problems of heredity and environment. Furthermore, as Clarke held, if the will is free, it is nevertheless limited. It is narrower in its sphere than life, and its power is weakened by lack of harmony among man's own powers. Man has misused his freedom, disabling himself to a degree that renders him unable to effect his own renovation without assistance from the Holy Spirit.

Still, on the whole, optimism about man persisted. Said Clarke:

Humanity certainly is by nature a slowly rising race, with a native tendency to outgrow faults. Sin is of course a burden and a clog upon that upward tendency, and one that might become so heavy as to nullify all higher possibilities. But God has certainly endowed humanity with a tendency to rise, which is only another way of saying that nature is favorable to goodness.[26]

This is so because an " ought " is built into the very constitution of man: " The law of human nature requires conformity to the perfect goodness, the character of God." [27] This " ought " has its source, not in the will of God but in the nature and character of God, and thus — since God and man are kin in Clarke's view — in the nature and character of man. " Obligation . . . is grounded at once in the nature of man and in the nature of God, and both because it is grounded in the nature of rational existence." [28]

Clarke was not insensible, nor were other liberals, to the fact that man's moral agency implies a limitation upon the divine will and action.

But God has created spirits intelligent and free, with a constitution that implies moral agency. He has given them certain power to do their will, even though it be opposed to him. By such creative action God has limited himself. He would otherwise have had the only will in the universe; but he has called other wills into being, and given to each one a limited field of genuine sovereignty. Their action is their own, with the responsibility and the consequences.[29]

D. The liberals held to an emphatic personalism.

The pervasive liberal refrain of the primacy of personal values and emphasis upon the development of personality has one of its roots in evolution and another in the growing popular sentiment for democracy in the nineteenth century. It has already been noted above that the liberals thought of personality as the end product of the evolutionary process and believed that the personal — some talked of the spiritual — is the deepest reality within the natural process even before personality itself emerges in explicit form. Personalism was also a note consistently struck in the influential German theology: Ritschl writing of his " assured conviction that human life is of more worth than all the world," and Harnack identifying " the infinite value of the human soul " as one of the central elements in the gospel.

William Newton Clarke insisted that God has a spiritual purpose for the universe, and that purpose is to create spirits and to make them perfect. " The personality of Jesus," said Walter Rauschenbusch, " is a call to the emancipation of our own personalities." [30]

Personality was seen by the liberals as the essential key to understanding God's nature and led to their practice of speaking of God as Father. Rauschenbusch hailed this view of God's character as one of the supreme religious achievements of Jesus:

> When he took God by the hand and called him " our Father," he democratized the conception of God. He disconnected the idea from the coercive and predatory state, and transferred it to the realm of family life, the chief social embodiment of solidarity and love. He not only saved humanity; he saved God. He gave God his first chance of being loved and of escaping from the worst misunderstandings conceivable.[31]

Shailer Mathews wrote:

> God must be either the personalized Whole or, as I am forced rather to believe, the Person who, as over against our own personalities, expresses Himself in the Whole. No religion can ever suffice that makes Him anything less than ourselves. And we are persons.[32]

Mathews was later to go even farther by defining God as "the personality-producing forces of the cosmos." He did not intend thereby to reduce God himself to impersonal natural process, since he also insisted that personality-producing forces are themselves capable of personal response.

If many of the emphases of liberal theology were not congenial to G. B. Foster, whose more radical theological construction grew increasingly separated from the historic evangelical faith, he nevertheless shared this personalistic enthusiasm. For Foster, the agency to be employed in salvation

> is not now "sound doctrine," so much as sound personalities. As fire kindles fire, and not some theory about the nature of flame, so persons save persons. Thus revelation is the content of holy personalities whose base and roots are God, not of sacred doctrines.[33]

In identifying the uniqueness of Jesus, Foster wrote:

> What was new was certainly the disposition and self-consciousness of Jesus. From these there gradually grew up in his soul a value-judgment that was new also, namely, that not *things,* not even *sacred* things, but that *persons only* are worthful. Faith in the infinite worth of the human personality in the sight of God — if there was anything new in the thought of Jesus, it was this.[34]

Thus for Foster, a Christian "is one who knows God in the man Jesus, one for whom Jesus is the personality which determines his relation to God." [35]

E. Liberals universally affirmed the centrality of Jesus Christ.

Indeed, if the nondoctrinal center of the liberal movement is to be found in the evolutionary world view, the doctrinal center is surely to be found in its common and constant Christological preoccupation. It was common for the liberals, from Smyth to Rauschenbusch, to describe the essence of Christianity by reference to Christ. In this they found strong support in German theology, as we have already seen. In Schleiermacher's thought, the uniqueness of Christ was affirmed as fulfilling a generally adduced principle of adequacy and finality — Christ is the supreme instance of the unrefracted God-consciousness. In the Ritschlian tradition, God's revelation in Christ was taken to be unique and final, in the sense that we can apply no categories to its explanation prior to the revelation itself. It is revelation, and not some previously adduced principle, that discloses the real nature of the divine life, in Ritschl's view. In either case, the central importance of Jesus Christ is reverently acknowledged.

William Adams Brown declared that the most important contribution of modern theology to the equipment of the preacher is renewed emphasis upon Christ as the only center and norm of Christianity. He is the founder of Christianity; he is the standard of the Christian religion; he is the organizing principle of the Christian movement.[36] When William Newton Clarke cited the two sources of Christian theology as the revelation of God in Jesus Christ and the universe (including man and nature), he made his priority unmistakably clear:

> Shall Christian theology first learn what it can of God from the world and man, and then come at last to Christ as the highest source of knowledge? No. This is exactly what Christian theology is not compelled to do. Christ is the first source, not the second. . . . The best of all revelations of God has been made in Christ, and rendered available to men of the modern age, and with this Christian theology is entitled to begin.[37]

Said Shailer Mathews, " For my part I am perfectly ready to substitute something better for the gospel as soon as it appears, but I am as yet unable to imagine anything more final than the religion of Jesus as found in the New Testament." [38] George Burman Foster, at his growing distance from the main stream of liberalism, nevertheless insisted that the essence of Christianity is Christ. He admitted that we do not know many details of Jesus' life and teaching.

> But nothing concerning him of which critical inquiry can make us uncertain is an object of religious faith. . . . Thus, too, it is the human Jesus *as expression of the personal life of God* that faith craves and criticism allows. It is the personality of Jesus for which faith cares — cares, however, because in Jesus we find as nowhere else existing revelation of the divine will and a nowhere else postulated aim of human life.[39]

Walter Rauschenbusch was perhaps typical of the liberals in viewing Jesus as " the perfect religious personality, a spiritual life completely filled by the realization of a God who is love." [40] That personality was a supreme spiritual achievement. It was won by Jesus, not received as a divine endowment. " The personality which he achieved was a new type of humanity. Having the power to master and assimilate others, it became the primal cell of a new social organism." [41] So by the process of cellular reproduction and division, by growth slow but inexorable, the spiritual influence of Jesus has worked its way into the body of humanity with astonishing consequence.

The full greatness of the problem of Jesus strikes us when we see him in his connection with human history. Our own consciousness of God's love and forgiveness, our inward freedom, our social feeling, the set of our will toward the achievement of the Kingdom of God, our fellowship with the " two or three " in which we have a realization of the higher presence, we owe to our connection with the historical force Jesus initiated.[42]

Nor was Rauschenbusch concerned to explain this power of Jesus in the traditional Christological language of the creeds and councils. " The social gospel," he insisted,

is not primarily interested in metaphysical questions; its christological interest is all for a real personality who could set a great historical process in motion; it wants his work interpreted by the purposes which ruled and directed his active life; it would have more interest in basing the divine quality of his personality on free and ethical acts of his will than in dwelling on the passive inheritance of a divine essence.[43]

One of the most characteristic preoccupations of the liberals was the distinction between " the religion *of* Jesus " and " the religion *about* Jesus." The historic creeds and confessions of Christendom, in some degree anticipated by the Pauline theology, had succeeded, in the liberal view, only in establishing a lifeless orthodoxy that offered a denatured Christ clothed in the vestments of Hellenistic metaphysical speculation. The problem, then, was to find the real man behind the theology, and having found him, to follow him. If the religion *about* Jesus demanded dogmatic assent to propositions about his deity, the religion *of* Jesus demanded imitation of his humanity. It was possible to live the Christlike life precisely because for many the humanity of Jesus was seen as continuous with the humanity of all men. George A. Gordon, in predicting the direction faith was to take in the future, said:

It is expected that the humanity of Jesus Christ will become more and more controlling in all thinking about the character of God and the nature and destiny of man. . . . Jesus is not an alien in man's world. In him more than in any other that world comes to know itself.[44]

The most popular and sentimentalized version of the theme of " following Jesus " was found in Charles Sheldon's novel of discipleship *In His Steps* (1897); and the fact that Sheldon's book was one of the all-time " best sellers " with an estimated twenty million copies circulated testifies to the tenacity and durability of the theme.

If there was a tendency among some liberals to stress the continuity of Jesus with the generality of mankind, others wanted to claim for him a more radical uniqueness. So William Newton Clarke insisted that Jesus was not formed out of the common stock. His was " clean humanity," formed by an immediate act of God. It is impossible, said Clarke, to separate that humanity from divinity. The spirit that constituted the personality of Jesus was divine. The fact that that spirit lived within human limitations rendered his personality human. The incarnation was not necessitated by man's sin but rather represented God's eternal purpose to unite himself with man. It is the work of Jesus Christ to bring man into moral unity and fellowship with God.

The Incarnation was possible because God and man are alike; yet it was rendered possible by the greatness that belongs to God alone. The way was opened by the constitution of man; but the power to enter humanity dwelt in that greatness of God which man does not share.[45]

Henry Ward Beecher insisted that Christ

has mystery above him, and speaks truths that are out of our reach; he gives evidence in his appearance, in his conversation and in his discourses, of one who is familiar with the upper, spiritual, and invisible sphere, and who is attempting, by his life and teaching, to interpret it in the lower, physical and visible sphere. So there is in the life of Christ a manifestation of divinity; a double consciousness. . . .[46]

F. Liberal religion was thoroughly ethicized religion.

Walter Rauschenbusch put the matter forthrightly when he wrote:

Every step in the historical evolution of religion has been marked by a closer union of religion and ethics and by the elimination of non-ethical religious performances. This union of religion and ethics reached its highest perfection in the life and mind of Jesus. . . . It is clear that our Christianity is most Christian when religion and ethics are viewed as inseparable elements of the same single-minded and whole-hearted life, in which the consciousness of God and the consciousness of humanity blend completely.[47]

This ethical emphasis was a part of the liberal program for simplifying Christianity, which the liberals thought of as the rescue of faith from the obscure irrelevancies of theological speculation. Washington Gladden, then, could insist that

to be a Christian means simply to follow Christ — "to accept as the ruling axiom of ethical conduct the command that a man shall love his neighbor as himself" — and the way to begin is just to begin. All disturbing questions of ability and inability, of election and condemnation, can be laid to one side.[48]

The ethical ideal was most often described by the liberals in terms of the law of love and the Kingdom of God. In this, of course, they found inspiring precedent in the Ritschlians. Ritschl himself had written:

In the idea of God as the final goal of all things lies the reason why Jesus recognises as binding upon Himself for God's sake the widest conceivable aim of moral effort, namely, the union of mankind through love. . . . Inasmuch as Jesus desired His own attitude to God to be shared by the rest of mankind, He laid upon His disciples, as their aim also, the union of mankind through love, or, in other words, the realisation of the Kingdom of God.[49]

The whole matter became the more simplified when Harnack declared the kernel of Jesus' teaching to include " the kingdom of God and its coming " and " the commandment of love and the higher righteousness."

In American liberalism all this came to its classical expression in the thought of Walter Rauschenbusch, for whom salvation was " the voluntary socializing of the soul." [50] The Kingdom of God was understood as " humanity organized according to the will of God." [51] The doctrine of the Kingdom, said Rauschenbusch, " is absolutely necessary to establish that organic union between religion and morality, between theology and ethics, which is one of the characteristics of the Christian religion." [52] In this Rauschenbusch was joined by Shailer Mathews, who defined the content of the Christian gospel in this way:

The gospel is a message of the redemptive love of the God of Law; of God's presence in Jesus; of a spiritual and therefore more individual life beyond death made possible by the transformation of the repentant human personality by dynamic personal union with the God of Love mediated by faith in Jesus; and of a regenerate society that shall bring blessing to the individual because of the socialization of the regenerate spiritual life of individuals, — all revealed as realizable and morally just by the supreme teaching, the spiritual experiences, the sinless life, the death and resurrection of the historical Jesus, and further guaranteed by the spiritual experience of his followers who accept the message as true and make it controlling in their own lives.[53]

In G. B. Foster, the key role of the Kingdom as a social reality disappeared. He thinks of it simply as " the nearness of God." But he is no less insistent than Rauschenbusch and Mathews on the primacy of love. " It is this love, *and this alone,* that Jesus says is required of man." [54] And it is, for Foster, the supreme personal embodiment of love in Jesus that gives to the Christian religion its finality.

It must be noted — partly because the liberals themselves drew attention to it — that there is a clear connection between the new view of the ethical imperative and the development in the nineteenth century of the broadening democratization of life, politically and otherwise. Recall the striking statement of Rauschenbusch that when Jesus " took God by the hand and called him ' our Father,' he democratized the conception of God." Gerald Birney Smith notes, more analytically but with approval, that " one who compares the theological treatises of today with those of a century or more ago cannot fail to be struck with the very considerable modifications which have been made at the behest of this democratic ideal." [55]

One of the distinctive features of the ethical note of liberalism, as contrasted with an earlier pietism for example, is its insistence upon the direct relevance of Christian imperatives not simply to individual morality but to social and institutional morality. This, of course, is the main burden of the social gospel, but that relevance is also asserted by those who stood outside the social gospel movement, most strikingly those who were identified with the individualism and moralism which characterized the gospel of wealth.[56] So Henry Ward Beecher could insist that " it is the duty of the minister of the gospel to preach on every side of political life. I do not say that he *may;* I say that he *must.*" [57] To be sure, the practical program whereby this emphasis on institutional morality worked itself out differed markedly within the liberal movement — the men of the gospel of wealth tended to give sanction to existing institutional mores; the men of the social gospel, on the other hand, sought to topple those mores by utilizing the revolutionary energies of social protest. Both groups were united, however, in discerning a social imperative in the gospel.

G. Liberals insisted on the legitimacy of applying the test of rational intelligibility to Biblical and doctrinal matters, as to every other phase of knowledge and experience.

In this they were doubtless appropriating the confidence in reason that emerged in the Enlightenment and that was strengthened by the demonstration of the widening grasp and scope of man's critical powers in scientific investigation.

Reason, as the liberals used the term, was neither the rather abstract rationalism of an earlier scholasticism, nor yet the rather sharply delimited objective methodology of science. Reason, as Theodore Munger wrote in defining the New Theology, is to have

> a somewhat larger and broader use . . . than has been accorded to theology. And by reason we do not mean mere speculation nor a formal logic, but that full exercise of our nature which embraces the intuitions, the conscience, the susceptibilities, and the judgment, i.e., man's whole inner being.[58]

The consequence of this for Munger is that "we accept the Christian faith because of the reasonableness of its entire substance, and not because we have somehow become persuaded that a revelation has been made." [59] That statement is too extreme to characterize some of the liberals, but if they did not give up the primacy of revelation, they nevertheless expressed their confidence that what God gives in revelation will commend itself to human reason.

George A. Gordon declared that the essential trustworthiness of the human mind must be taken for granted. The great secret of Jesus for Gordon is that "he is himself absolutely sane," which means that the rational and moral vision are one in him.[60] Newell Dwight Hillis expressed his confidence in the human judgment as "an instrument testing things invisible." [61] William Adams Brown wrote that modern science has increased our faith in the trustworthiness of our own faculties and the intelligibility of the universe. He went even farther and suggested that rationality is the common spiritual element that unites man and God.[62] Shailer Mathews proceeded upon his apologetic task with the attempt to show, not so much that the Christian gospel is true in itself, as that it is reasonable from the point of view of modern man, and he counted on man to be able to discern the presence of God in the world by the use of his own faculties, and called men to trust the impulses and potencies of their own spiritual life.[63] Shirley Jackson Case, in discussing "The Historical Method in the Study of Religion," insisted that truth carries its own attestation, which meant that the human mind is such that it is capable of discerning and appropriating that self-evidence.[64]

The obvious corollary of the trustworthiness of human reason is confidence in the rational intelligibility of all life and experience. It is the coincidence of human faculty (rational intelligence) and world (rational order) that creates the confidence of liberalism. So, to speak of the legitimacy of applying the test of rational intelligibility to Biblical and doctrinal matters, as to every other phase of knowledge and experience, is to assert the authority of experience. Christian doctrine is the product of human experience, the liberals never tired of insisting; it emerges out of living situations. The Bible attests itself to us by virtue of its abiding human experiences and in spite of its outmoded categories. The language here is Fosdick's in *The Modern Use of the Bible,* but the principle of distinguishing between experience and Biblical category was urged by the men of the New Theology long before Fosdick gave it memorable statement. The human life of Jesus gave confidence that the spiritual truths, which he taught and livingly embodied, could be confirmed and validated by the universal witness of human experience.

This prominence given to experience was supported in different ways by both Schleiermacher and Ritschl. The former located genuine religion in the universal and distinctively religious experience of absolute dependence, and the latter insisted on both the possibility and the necessity that Jesus become a part of the believer's own historical environment — which is to say, a part of his own personal experience — before genuine communion with God could take place.

As a result of this emphasis on experience, the liberals characteristically issued a call for an experimental religion. This was an attempt to appropriate for Christian faith the objective certainty that was seen to be building up in scientific investigation. Leighton Williams spoke for many when he declared that Christianity has a scientific platform of its own, on the basis of which the Christian proceeds in his knowledge of spiritual truth along the same lines as the scientific investigator. The main difference between the two, said Williams, is their respective fields of investigation.[65] The truth of Christianity, echoed William Newton Clarke — that the affirmations of Christianity accord with fact and that it sets forth the great spiritual realities — needs nothing but " the test of genuine experiment " for its proof.[66] So, declared Walter Rauschenbusch, " the more scientific our religious life becomes, the closer, somehow, does it come to Jesus." [67] Shirley Jackson Case could insist that the truth of Christianity is not to be established on the basis of infallible authority. Communion with God is not

> conditioned by special displays of the divine initiative, nor is it to be obtained at present by any one set of specific prescriptions. It is available for every individual on a strictly empirical basis.[68]

One could claim, then, that the men of the gospel of wealth represented the most crass expression of the claim for an experimental religion, when they drew a direct line from religious virtue to wealth and from sin to indigence.

H. Liberals applied the tools of scientific, literary, and historical scholarship to the study of the Bible.

This is a special instance of three preceding characteristics — continuity, rational intelligibility, and experiential method. In the liberal view, it was possible to apply scientific, literary, and historical tools to the Biblical literature, because that literature is subject to the same laws of development as any other literary corpus. So, said Theodore Munger, the New Theology seeks to interpret the Scriptures in " a more natural way." It reads the Scriptures as literature without derogating their inspiration. Thus the Bible is to be understood, according to Munger, as purely instrumental rather than magical; " it is not a revelation, but it is the history of a revelation." [69] Furthermore, said William Newton Clarke, the Bible is not so simple to interpret as the more traditional view of inspiration would suggest.

> The fact is that absolutely perfect understanding of what a writer meant by a written page can never be obtained. Even the more external matters cannot be managed to perfection. Perfect translation is impossible. The meaning of words and the structure of sentences

can never be so determined that there shall be no ambiguity whatever, and the historical setting can never be perfectly reproduced in the reader's mind. But even farther beyond reach is the inner work of interpretation. One man cannot perfectly take another's point of view and think his thought after him: least of all can this be done when the other speaks out of another age and training, thinking his thought in a world of personal experience which to the student does not exist.

Facing these patent difficulties, Clarke concluded, we can only admit that

the Bible is a book that we can hope to understand as well as we need to understand it, through the best human endeavors with the help of God. In handling it we are free students, not required to agree with every statement we find.[70]

Walter Rauschenbusch summarized the critical approach to the Bible in these words:

The modern conception of inspiration not only recognizes the free operation and contributions of the distinctive psychical equipment of the inspired person, but seeks in every way to get beyond the individual to the social group which produced him, to the spiritual predecessors who inspired him, and to the audience which moved him because he hoped to move it.[71]

The practical result of the critical studies, said William Adams Brown, is to lay greater stress on the human element in the Bible's composition, and to insist that not all parts of the Bible are on the same moral and spiritual level. Rather than loss, this is gain for the modern Christian. This approach allows him to recover for spiritual use large sections of the Bible that had fallen into disuse. The Bible shows us men facing the same kinds of questions that contemporary men face, whose experience, therefore, can be practically helpful at the point where contemporary men most need help. But more than that, the older view of the Bible led to disunity, each man bringing to the book his own presuppositions. The new view calls us to judge the Bible by Christ, who is its center. For the supreme thing that the scientific study of the Bible accomplishes is to show us Christ in a more exact sense, in revealing his life and teaching in the Gospels. The older theology provided light, in its doctrine of the Holy Spirit, but direction is needed as well as light, and direction is supplied in the new clarity with which men are enabled to see Christ as a result of the critical study of the Bible. So William Adams Brown summarized the general liberal view.[72]

One thing that the liberals lacked — and it is scarcely surprising in view of their confidence in the scientific study of the Scripture — was an explicit doctrine of inspiration. Henry Ward Beecher extended the meaning of inspiration to a kind of universal category, writing that " it is *the human race* that has been inspired; and the Bible in every part of it was lived, first, and the record of it made afterwards." [73] In practical effect, then, the emphasis upon experimental religion and the authority of experience takes the place of the traditional doctrine of inspiration. Furthermore, there was in the liberals a confidence in the intuitive discernment of truth, and this too functioned in the place of an explicit theology of inspiration. So William Newton Clarke could write that theories of inspiration are destined to be left behind.

> We are now able to take the Bible as it is, and listen to its testimony, without first proving by a doctrine of inspiration that it must be listened to. At present a more interior and spiritual idea of the evidence of the present God may be applied. If God is in a book he will be found: we do not have to justify our sense of his presence there by building a theory to show how he got there. God shines by his own light.[74]

Clarke was not insensible to the dangers inherent in criticism. " The chief danger about the Bible at present," he wrote,

> is, on the one hand, that it will be studied too much in the mere spirit of criticism, without regard to its religious value, and, on the other, that the timidity of Christian people on critical grounds will prevent them from holding that religious value in its true rank and place.

Still, optimism overbalanced pessimism on the point, and Clarke could affirm that " by this time in the history of the world the quality of the Bible as the book of divine religion is so established that we may think of it with serene confidence." [75] In general, it is true, especially for liberals such as Clarke and Brown, that the Bible continued to hold a central place in the work of theology. For, said Brown, " it is the most ancient, direct and reliable source for our knowledge of the historic Christ, and . . . it is the most effective means for the awakening and stimulating of the present Christian life." [76]

If the liberals appropriated the methodological tools of the secular disciplines in their Biblical scholarship, it ought also to be noted that they appropriated the key scientific category of the time in their interpretation of Scripture. That category, of course, was evolution, and applied to the Bible, it yielded the idea of the presence within the Scriptures of a progressive revelation. " Thus," wrote Henry Ward Beecher,

> we find in the word of God there is an ascending development. The earliest periods are very simple. Men's thought of God was very simple and uncomplex. It grew more and more complex and loftier.[77]

To this there seemed to be unanimous agreement.

> God made special use of the Hebrew people, from Abraham, its father, in order gradually to manifest himself in his revelation with men; and when the fulness of time was come, he brought forth his Son Jesus Christ into the world, to complete the revelation that had been partially made before, by doing this supreme work of grace for the salvation of men. This progressive revelation is the basis of the Scriptures.[78]

Thus William Newton Clarke echoed Beecher.

I. The liberals were prepared to welcome both secular learning and secular comradeship in common causes.

Theodore Munger is an early and interesting example here. Two of his keenest interests were to relate theology to the university and to literature. He insisted that theological education should take place only in university centers, " that it might learn and adopt those careful and comprehensive habits of thought which are fostered by university life." He valued the restatements of Christianity made especially by the poets, whom he called, " the real defenders of the Faith." He traced the unrecognized theological implications in works of fiction. Munger wrote:

> The Christian value of an author is not to be determined by the fullness of his Christian assertion. . . . Christianity is all the while in need of two things: correction of its mistakes and perversions and development in the direction of its universality. None can do these two things so well as those who are partially outsiders. . . . In order to translate the natural into the divine, and to find a place for the divine in the natural, they who know the natural, and hold it even at some cost to the divine must be employed.[79]

William Newton Clarke wrote that he expected

> valuable help from the clear and straightforward thinking that is characteristic of the best intellectual work of our time. . . . Every advance in good intellectual practice helps Christian doctrine toward the day of disentanglement and independence.[80]

Of the secular social movement of the nineteenth century, Walter Rauschenbusch wrote:

> We refuse to regard it as a red-hot lava eruption from the crater of hell. We hold that it is a river flowing from the throne of God, sent by the Ruler of history for the purification of the nations. We see God's hand in it; we see Christ's blood in it; we see the creative energies of the Spirit in it, bringing out of its chaos the beauties of a new world.[81]

J. The liberal eschatology was essentially progressivistic and optimistic.

This optimism and progressivism were undoubtedly related to the progress made in science and technology and to the general cultural confidence engendered by social Darwinism. But it is also a product of the liberal apprehension of the gospel, with its world-redeeming power, and of the doctrine of the immanent God pervasively at work through the whole of creation. G. A. Gordon, writing of things to be expected, said:

The sense of humanity will more and more envelop all human interests, and among them the forms of religious belief. Humanity in the sense of a hierarchy of powers in the individual man, holding positions according to ideas of worth, with moral perception and moral feeling as sovereign; and humanity in the sense of an inclusive human brotherhood, where the good of each is seen to involve the good of all, and where the good of all can never be at the permanent sacrifice of any single soul, — this is the consciousness that is more and more to envelop the sum of man's interests.[82]

Washington Gladden exclaimed, " If it was ever worth while to live, it is worth while to live today. No better day than this has ever dawned on this continent. . . . What ought to be is going to be." [83] Wrote William Newton Clarke:

There is nothing but religious life that can most powerfully strengthen the cause of religion in the world. It is life that begets life. Only the genuine experience of the divine grace and life, — such experience as the first Christians had, and all the best of their successors, — only this can bring the help most needful. But I see it coming. Already, in our own time, we find a fresh insistence upon genuineness and reality in religion.[84]

Shailer Mathews declared that " the socialization of the gospel is proceeding, and that the plain man finds it easier today to embody the principles of Jesus than he did ten years ago." [85]

K. The liberals operated within a rather specific historical bias.

Their general futuristic orientation, plus their confidence in the ability of Biblical scholarship to disclose the essence of Christian history in the life and teachings of Jesus, meant that large segments of Christian history were ignored, if not deprecated and rejected. Harnack's influence is surely strong here, in his insistence that the development of Christian orthodoxy after the Biblical period represents an unfortunate hellenization of the gospel. Some, such as the Ritschlians, identified the Protestant Reformation with the repristinization of a perverted and polluted faith, and thus the sixteenth century was looked upon as a period of theological reformulation not unlike that in which the liberals themselves were engaged. It was common, however, to ignore Christian history before the Reformation, and to leap from the Reformation directly into the nineteenth century.

Henry Ward Beecher was one of the most violent in the rejection of the theological past. In *Evolution and Religion,* he wrote:

> The old theory of sin, then, — which will be exterminated, I think, by the new light thrown upon the origin of man and the conditions by which the race has developed, — is repulsive, unreasonable, immoral, and demoralizing. I hate it. I hate it because I love the truth, because I love God, and because I love my fellow-men. . . . People say to me, "It is generally understood that you are not a Calvinist." John Calvin can take care of himself. But I am a teacher of righteousness. I am a lover of mankind. . . . This whole theory of sin and its origin . . . is hideous, it is horrible, it is turning creation into a shambles and God into a slaughterer, and the human race into a condition worse a thousandfold than that of beasts.[86]

On another occasion, Beecher wrote:

> The chapters of the Westminster Confession of Faith concerning decrees, election, reprobation . . . , I regard as extraordinary specimens of *spiritual barbarism*. . . . I hold it to be a monster, and not a master of love, that is there portrayed.[87]

The violence of Beecher's language suggests that more is at issue here than the rejection of uncongenial ideas, especially in view of the fact that the heyday of Calvinism was long past by the time Beecher published his diatribe. Since history, in Beecher's view, is man's steady pilgrimage from the relative barbarism of every past to the relative enlightenment of every future, the rejection of the past was an act of piety, a sacrifice of primitive roots in the expectation of exalted ends.

Walter Rauschenbusch suggested that the new historical studies would emancipate men from "ancestor worship." [88] It has already been noted that William Newton Clarke omitted from his systematic theology virtually all dependence on Christian historical insight or reference to the historical development of the Christian faith. G. B. Foster expressed this historical bias in somewhat different terms when he wrote, "It is not a religion of facts, but of values; and values are timeless; that is, Christianity is an eternal religion which is *in,* but not *of,* the historical." [89]

Acknowledgment must be made here that many of the liberals did make frequent appeal to history. The Ritschlians particularly insisted upon the historical rootedness of the Christian revelation, and insisted, further, that Christ must become a part of the believer's own historical environment. But the historical bias of the Ritschlians comes in their rejection of the historical continuity of the Christian community, or, to put the matter somewhat more exactly, a rejection of the insights of the Christian community especially from the subapostolic period to the Reformation.

Others, like Mathews, insisted upon the primacy of the historical method in the study of Christianity. Yet the historical bias under which Mathews operated is disclosed in this quotation:

> Here is one characteristic of a positive, evangelical theology: it uses the material which theologies of the past have employed. It would throw away nothing which its analysis of the doctrinal development may discover to be more than concepts used to interpret eternal realities to a given age. But it starts with the strictly evangelic data which have been worked into the *corpus* of doctrine, rather than with that *corpus* itself.[90]

Here the last sentence is crucial — historical study is primarily extraction rather than appreciation.

L. The liberals insisted on the need for continuous theological reformulation and reinterpretation.

This is partly related to the tentativeness and experimentalism that was borrowed from science, and partly to the conviction that the rapid progress of human insight in the contemporary period " makes ancient good uncouth." So H. Shelton Smith wrote of Theodore Munger, that he

> drew a logical conclusion from this evolutionary idea of revelation: there can be no final formulation of the Christian faith; it must al-

ways remain in process of revision in order to keep step with a growing revelation.[91]

In looking to the future, William Newton Clarke predicted of the Christian faith that "it will take new forms, but it will be the old reality, and the Christian doctrine will stand forth strong and clear."[92]

Walter Rauschenbusch put the matter with characteristic directness: "Theology needs periodic rejuvenation. Its greatest danger is not mutilation but senility."[93]

Four THE VARIETIES OF LIBERALISM: THREE SIGNIFICANT VARIABLES

ADDED PRECISION for our definition of American Protestant liberalism will result from an examination of three variables that mark off significant differences among the liberals themselves. These differences are *methodological, ethical,* and *institutional.*

A. Methodologically, a distinction can be drawn between evangelicals and modernists within the liberal movement.

What Daniel Day Williams has said about certain later English theologians applies as well to the American theological development:

> The difference between Protestant modernism and certain Anglican figures (Gore, Temple) is that, while [the latter] are concerned to integrate Christian faith with modern thought, still they finally stand with the revelation which is guarded by the creeds as over against human experience and reason. But Protestant modernism was more radical; it said that even the Creed must be validated with our religious experience and reason.[1]

The methodological starting point for evangelical liberalism was invariably the revelation of God in Jesus Christ. William Newton Clarke, as we have already seen, made it quite clear that, although Christ and the world are the two sources of Christian theology, Christ is the primary source. If rational and empirical experience validate Christian faith, as Clarke was sure they do, they are, nevertheless, not the source of that faith. "A Christian," Clarke wrote, is not obliged to work his way up toward knowledge of God by the long and weary course by which humanity has approached it; not first through nature, or even through the partial revelations of the Old Covenant, are we to learn God, but directly from Christ. A Christian has been born into the day; he has not to wait and learn what day is, by watching for the dawn and seeing the day break. The best of all revelations of God has been made in Christ, and rendered available to men of the modern age, and with this Christian theology is entitled to begin. In the light that streams from Christ it is permited to do its work.[2]

Clarke's definition of the Christian religion is unequivocally Christocentric, and somewhat reminiscent of Schleiermacher's:

Christianity is a religion, inasmuch as it is one of the forms taken by the life of man in his relations with God. It differs from other religions in this, that its conception of God and of man's relation to him, and its impulse and power for the religious life, are derived from a self-revelation of God in human history, which culminated in Jesus Christ; and that it is under the influence of that revelation that the Christian religious life is lived.[3]

So far was Walter Rauschenbusch from yielding faith in the primacy of Christ to the results of scientific scholarship that he actually discerned in science an antagonism toward the Christian revelation. In an address on " Religion the Life of God in the Soul of Man," Rauschenbusch wrote that

in the face of Nature as we know her, it is a tremendous affirmation to assert that God is not only just, but that he is love. For myself I need all the assurance contained in the self-consciousness of Jesus Christ to brace my faith. That popular conviction of the love of God and of the consequent goodness of the world shows how much humanity owes to Jesus. Without the historical contribution he has made to human thought and feeling, I do not see how, in the present state of scientific knowledge, that conviction could stand up against the total impression left by the natural sciences.[4]

Shailer Mathews and George Burman Foster, who helped to prepare the way for the " Chicago school " of Christian naturalism, and who held contemporary scientific scholarship in the highest regard, nevertheless insisted upon the primacy of a Christocentric faith. In an article on " A Positive Method for an

Evangelical Theology " written in 1909, Mathews called for a positive theology that is frankly evangelical, " i.e., that utilizes methodically the gospel as given by biblical theology." [5] A year later in an examination of *The Gospel and Modern Man,* he asserted that

social evolution enlightened by the Christian church would teach us it is better to live in accordance with the supposition that a God of Law is a God of Love, that individual development is not to be stopped short of death, that the spiritual order is superior to the natural, and that a better community is yet to be formed. But, apologetically strong as such a daring . . . position may be, it is weak indeed when compared with the same teachings backed by an assurance of the trustworthiness of the evangelic picture of a genuinely historical Jesus, the concrete expression of the supremacy of the spiritual life.[6]

Foster was, if anything, more determinedly Christocentric than Mathews. In an article on " Christianity and Modern Culture " written in 1909, he asserted:

Trusting to the judgment of historical science and not to the judgment of religious enthusiasm, Jesus loses his place in the religion of the Christian. He is sacrificed to skepticism. . . . Men who have thought long and deeply upon this subject now see that it is at once irreligious and disastrous to found our faith upon the conclusions of historical science concerning Jesus. To that science the nonexistence of the Jesus of history is now — and probably henceforth — admittedly a possibility. It is a question of finding God in the biblical portrait — historical or not — of the Christ, and if God was once there he is there still: not there alone, but there, there as nowhere else in the world. This judgment of faith is incommensurable with, and wholly independent of, the judgment of criticism — relying on which we are irremediably doomed to skepticism, not to religion. . . .[7]

In a volume of lectures published posthumously under the editorship of D. C. Macintosh, Foster described his own theological method in these terms:

. . . in dogmatic work we have to lay hold of the earthly person and work of the Savior, Jesus Christ, as the center of the whole revelation of God and as the starting-point of the independent certainty of faith and the inner understanding of faith.[8]

In ways other than theological method, the evangelical liberals preserved the historic faith: (1) " They distinguished themselves from their liberal contemporaries," H. Richard Niebuhr has written, " by keeping relatively close to evangelical notions of the sovereignty of God, of the reign of Christ and of the coming kingdom." [9] (2) There was a strong consciousness of sin among them. Indeed, Walter Rauschenbusch insisted that " any religious tendency or school of theology must be tested by the question whether it does justice to the religious consciousness of sin." [10] If some modern theologians wanted to discard the doctrine of original sin, Rauschenbusch was prepared to defend it, because " it is one of the few attempts of individualistic theology to get a solidaristic view of its field of work." [11] To be sure, the old theology must be rejected where it tries to involve us in the sin of Adam and " fix on us all a uniform corruption," [12] but original sin is to be affirmed where it

> views the race as a great unity, descended from a single head, and knit together through all ages by unity of origin and blood. This natural unity is the basis and carrier for the transmission and universality of sin. Depravity of will and corruption of nature are transmitted wherever life itself is transmitted.[13]

William Newton Clarke described sin as " the abiding habit of the human race," entering through the early acceptance of evil by the free will of man, and perpetuated by means of the race connection.[14] William Adams Brown insisted that " nothing more hopeless can be said either of an individual or a society than that it has lost its sense of sin." [15] (3) Salvation was not understood by the evangelicals as adjustment but as regeneration. In spite of his conviction about the social character of sin, Rauschenbusch had no confidence in sociological remedies for it. Instead, he called for conversion, " a break with our own sinful past." [16] What is required is " a change which turns a man from self to God and humanity." [17] " In our unregenerate condition," he wrote,

> the consciousness of God is weak, occasional, and suppressed. The more Jesus Christ becomes dominant in us, the more does the light

and life of God shine readily in us, and create a religious personality which we did not have. Life is lived under a new synthesis.[18]

We have already noted above how, in the view of William Newton Clarke, man has misused his freedom, disabling himself to a degree that renders him unable to effect his own renovation without assistance from the Holy Spirit. (4) The work of Christ, therefore, is to convict man of sin and awaken him to faith. Clarke's language here was quite orthodox:

Christ is the gift of the heart of God, who desires to save the world. He comes to make known to men the true God, to infuse spirituality into their being, and thus to give them eternal life. In other words, he comes to seek and find lost men, and gather them into the kingdom of righteousness, where instead of living in sin they shall do the holy will of God as his children.[19]

Rauschenbusch was inclined to stress the significance of Christ as the New Adam, the progenitor of a new humanity:

The personality which he achieved was a new type in humanity. Having the power to master and assimilate others, it became the primal cell of a new social organism. Even if there had been no sin from which mankind had to be redeemed, the life of Jesus would have dated an epoch in the consequently new social standards. He is the real revelation of God. Other conceptions have to be outlived; his has to be attained.[20]

(5) The evangelical liberals maintained a realistic doctrine of the Holy Spirit. The Spirit, said Clarke, is God working in the spirit of man, and accomplishing the results that are sought in the mission and work of Christ. This Spirit is no mere influence but is God himself, personally present as Spirit in contact with human spirits.[21] Said Rauschenbusch:

A religious man knows that he has no merit of his own, and that all his righteousness was wrought in him by God. To suppose that he can set his own will on God and work out his own salvation is sub-Christian. . . . To suppose that we can work out a living knowledge of the truth from a sacred book without the enlightening energy of the spirit of God is sub-Christian and rationalistic. On the other hand, to be conscious of the divine light, to listen to the inner voice, to read the inspired words of the Bible with an answering glow of fire, is part of the consciousness of God to which we are entitled.[22]

The methodological starting point for modernism, in contrast, was modern knowledge and experience, by which all claims of revelation or authoritative tradition were to be tested. The modernist was a Christian who affirmed much that was contained in the evangelical faith, but rather than moving from Christ to culture, the modernist moved from culture to Christ. Typically, the modernist affirmed the ultimacy of the Christian religion and the final authority of Jesus for the spiritual life, but he usually arrived at those value judgments as a result of what he took to be the evidence arising out of scientific investigation or social experience. That is, the norms for religious truth were drawn from the presumed empirical data — less often from philosophical speculation — and the Christian faith was then affirmed to be in some way the fulfillment of those norms. The assumption of the modernist, then, was that by this objective methodology anyone who submitted himself to disciplined examination of the empirical evidence on the nature of reality, human and otherwise, could reasonably be expected to arrive at the same conclusion concerning the finality of the Christian religion.

Modernism on these terms was a post-World War I development. No major figure of the liberal movement before 1917 qualifies for designation as a modernist.

The liberals to whom attention is given in this study were, for the most part, men of amazing longevity. Henry Ward Beecher died in 1887 at the age of 73; all the others survived the turn of the century: Theodore Munger (1830–1910), William Newton Clarke (1841–1912), Washington Gladden (1836–1918), Newman Smyth (1843–1925), George Gordon (1853–1929), and Newell Dwight Hillis (1858–1929). Lyman Abbott, one of the most prominent spokesmen for a Christian evolutionary outlook, died in 1922 at the age of 86. Only Walter Rauschenbusch and George Burman Foster died prematurely, both in 1918, the former at the age of 57 and the latter at the age of 60. All of these were firmly within the evangelical camp. Even Foster, who perhaps had least in common with historic Christianity, had not become a modernist at the time of his death, as the evidence offered above has shown. William Adams Brown is one of the few evangelicals cited in this study who had a significant theological career after the war, and he continued an evangelical liberal to the end of his productive life.[23]

Shailer Mathews (1863–1941) and D. C. Macintosh (1877–1948) also had distinguished scholarly careers after World War I. Macintosh, although sometimes characterized as a modernist, was, in fact, an evangelical at heart. The task Macintosh set for himself was the development of theology as an empirical science. Since he defined religion as " a conscious relation . . . of active adjustment to the higher reality or power upon which man's highest values are believed ultimately to depend," [24] and God as " a Power not identifiable with ourselves, that makes for righteousness in and through us when we persist in the right religious adjustment," [25] he sought an experimental religion in which verified religious knowledge would result from the " right religious adjustment " to the " divine factor " in experience. This " divine factor " is discernible, he held, in those aspects of our experience which are value producing, but the experience of value is not sufficient in itself. To value experience is added the experience of the " numinous," and the coincidence of these constitutes the divine activity in human life.[26]

Macintosh believed that religious experimentation would require a discipline quite as rigorous as any scientific experimentation, including the following: (1) concentration of attention on the religious object and upon the values sought by the right religious adjustment; (2) self-surrender to the " divine factor " and active response to its working; and (3) persistence in concentration and self-surrender such that the right religious adjustment could conceivably bring about the desired consequences.[27] Out of such experimentation, Macintosh was confident that dependable and universal theological laws could be fashioned in relation to such matters as prayer, personal regeneration and conversion, peace with God, the awareness of personal guidance, and the assurance of forgiveness of sins.[28] Once he had succeeded in formulating these laws, he moved on to the development of a normative theological theory consisting of rational inferences from the laws.

> According to this normative theology, the transcendent God of faith has the same qualities of character as are dependably promoted in man through persistence in what we have called the right religious adjustment.

This is the basis, then, for the theological judgment that "God is holy love." [29]

Macintosh hoped that such a normative theology, based on theological laws resulting from the application of his experimental methodology to the problem of religious knowledge, would eventuate in a theological consensus to replace the traditional theological conflict that had characterized Christian history.

James A. Martin has noted that Macintosh's ability to create a genuine empirical theology was compromised by his own personal Christian commitment. What Macintosh thinks is universal and commonsense religion turns out, on closer examination, not to be the kind of universality and common sense on which science depends but only that of his own religious tradition.[30] Macintosh himself was not unaware of the distinctively Christian element in his work. He acknowledged Jesus of Nazareth as the supreme example of the right religious adjustment, much as Schleiermacher before him had found in Jesus the supreme instance of the God-consciousness. Schleiermacher was not embarrassed in making the figure of Jesus normative for the religious affections, since he was sure that Jesus was the best example of an awareness which needed to be awakened in every man. So Macintosh was not embarrassed to point to Jesus as the supreme instance of right religious adjustment to the pervasive working of that divine factor that awaited the response of all men. The divine dependability ensures that that which works in Jesus is available, upon fulfillment of appropriate conditions, to all men.

Thus, in spite of a pseudoscientific empiricism, Macintosh's theological methodology takes its start in the gospel. Since the presuppositions that he chose for empirical validation were most often drawn from the religious experience of Jesus, George F. Thomas is probably right in saying that in his " theological laws " Macintosh only succeeded in rationalizing the conventional views of an evangelical liberalism.[31]

Evidence has already been presented in support of the contention that Shailer Mathews, in his prewar writings, consistently employed the evangelical methodology. Two publications that appeared in 1924, however, made it clear that he was by then moving progressively out of the evangelical camp.

In *The Faith of Modernism,*[32] he described with evident enthusiasm " the projection of the Christian movement into modern conditions." Modernism, said Mathews, is by no means independent of the community of faith; rather, " it proceeds within the religious limits set by an ongoing Christian group." Indeed, modernists are evangelical Christians who accept Jesus Christ as God's saving revelation, but modernism attempts to separate Christian experience from its historically conditioned and, therefore, outmoded doctrinal expressions, in the interest of giving that experience new relevance in the contemporary world. The modernist believes that Christianity can meet the spiritual and moral needs of the world because of his conviction that Christianity is consistent with other realities.

As Mathews defined it, modernism " is the use of the methods of science to find, state and use the permanent and central values of inherited orthodoxy in meeting the needs of the modern world." Modernists are, therefore, to be distinguished from other Christians by their distinctive methodology, especially in contrast to the dogmatists. The latter want to reassert the past in the interest of theological regularity, while the former utilize the scientific method in the interest of more efficient religious development. The modernist is a critic and a historian before he is a theologian, and he has implicit trust in the historical method as a special form of the scientific method. By the use of that method, the modernist expects to discover the permanent values of Christianity.

Incidentally, Mathews rejected Unitarianism on the same ground that he rejected Confessionalism, namely, that it is a form of theological rationalism and therefore inadequate in meeting the religious needs of contemporary men.

If, in this book on modernism, Mathews still purported to stand in continuity with the evangelical faith, his theological method was, nevertheless, in process of significant modification. Whereas the evangelicals trusted in the power of the Christian revelation itself to confirm its own permanent value, Mathews expected to discover that permanent value by means of historical and scientific investigation, which is to say that the norms of truth are now defined independently of revelation. Christianity was described as " consistent with other realities," which implies that it was to be tested, at least in part, by its cohesiveness with those realities whose status had been determined apart from the Christian revelation. If Mathews was not yet a modernist by our definition of the term, he was, at least, well on the way.

Contributions of Science to Religion [33] appeared in the same year as *The Faith of Modernism* and gave emphatic confirmation to that development. This volume consisted of essays written by thirteen scholars from the natural and social sciences, which Mathews edited and to which he added four chapters of his own. The existence of God, said Mathews, is as assured an inference of empirical science as is ether, and for the same reason — it alone provides an adequate and unifying explanation for observed phenomena. More than this, science is providing new content for the idea of God. The view of God held by traditional religion was the product of social life and technique. It raised to a transcendent level man's experience of a power upon which he is dependent. Thus, orthodoxy has typically described God in political terms. But science, Mathews insisted, is now giving us a new organizing concept for our understanding of God — " that reciprocal relationship of the universe and the atom, the evironment and the organism to which science is accustoming thought." From a scientific point of view, then,

> religion is thus seen to be life in accord with an increasingly rational working hypothesis based on something other than *a priori* reasoning or ecclesiastical authority. It draws its content and its legitimacy from both knowledge and experience. Religious values are a part of our social heritage tested by experiment.[34]

Mathews believed that he saw emerging out of the new science a new religion, even more faithful to the teaching of Jesus than the old, and to this new religion he was confident that the future belonged.

> Its sympathies are social rather than individual, and its theology is based not on metaphysics of the Godhead interpreted by human analogy but on those judgments of value and those undeniable facts of science which seem to condition all self-expression.[35]

If the method of modernism did not become controlling in Mathews' theological work until after the war, it was nevertheless, anticipated in his earlier writings. A dozen years before the two volumes above appeared, he had published an article in *The American Journal of Sociology* on " The Social Origins of Theology " in which he argued that theology is a social product based on the dramatic and dynamic presuppositions which the community of faith " has unconsciously accepted as the basis of social values." [36] Orthodox Jewish and Christian theology alike were " transcendentalized politics " on this view, adequate enough, perhaps, in their own time but impotent in the modern world.[37] The work of theological reconstruction, therefore, must seek to identify " the theological schema which came over from the messianic Christianity of the primitive church and . . . evaluate the schema itself in terms of religious efficiency." [38] Just as theology in earlier epochs had " utilized the dynamic presuppositions conditioning all social activity in general," an adequate theology for the modern period will " seek to utilize such presuppositions as are now creative." [39]

It is significant for his later development that in this essay Mathews assigned no place in his analysis to revelation, and when revelation is denied an independent status, the evangelical element in theology is on the way to dissolution. A dozen years later, reflecting on this development in his autobiography, Mathews wrote:

I increasingly felt that my approach to religious reconstruction should be from the point of view of an existing religious group rather than from that of abstract philosophical thought. The Christianity with which I was concerned was not so much the essence of truth as the organized Christian movement which carried forward permanent values in its beliefs. It was only gradually that the current of my thinking led to decreased emphasis upon evangelical formulas.[40]

The evangelical is to be thought of as the central tradition of liberalism, both because it stands in the most direct continuity with the classical Christian faith and because it consistently produced the most influential figures, not only in the period under study but in the postwar era as well. The name of Harry Emerson Fosdick, to recall only one of the postwar evangelicals, came almost to be synonymous with the liberal movement, and he was surely its most illustrious public spokesman throughout his preaching career.[41] That evangelical liberalism increasingly yielded to modernism is perhaps not surprising. In *The Kingdom of God in America,* H. Richard Niebuhr spoke of the evangelical as the " mediating " position and commented:

No mediating theology in history has ever been able to keep in balance the opposing elements it seeks to reconcile, and this truth held for the American mediators also. As time went on liberalism began to outweigh Evangelicalism more and more. At the same time the former tended to become increasingly secular, or to speak more accurately, to lose the sense of the broken relation between God and man, between the present and the coming kingdom. In the course of succeeding generations the heritage of faith with which liberalism had started was used up.[42]

B. Ethically, a distinction can be made among the liberals depending upon whether they took an accommodationist or a transformationist view of culture.

The accommodationists were those who advocated a " gospel of wealth " in which man's acquisitive drives and powers, given institutional expression and cultural sanction by a rapidly growing and relatively uncontrolled industrial capitalism, were declared to be ordained by God as the instruments of personal and social good.[43]

The " gospel of wealth " was a term coined by industrialist Andrew Carnegie in an article entitled " Wealth " published in the *North American Review* in 1889. Carnegie argued that modern capitalistic society had four foundations — individualism, private property, the law of accumulation of wealth, and the law of competition. These foundations " are the highest result of human experience, the soil in which society, so far, has produced the best fruit." Carnegie was prepared to admit that there may be some inequity and imperfection in the practical expression of these foundations, but they are, nevertheless,

> the best and the most valuable of all that humanity has yet accomplished. . . . But whether the law [of competition] be benign or not, we must say of it. . . . It is here; we cannot evade it; no substitutes for it have been found; and while the law may sometimes be hard on the individual, it is best for the race, because it ensures the survival of the fittest in every department. *We accept and welcome, therefore, as conditions to which we must accommodate ourselves,* great inequality of environment; the concentration of business, industrial and commercial, in the hands of the few; and the law of competition between these, as being not only beneficial, but essential to the future progress of the race.[44]

Once having acquired wealth, Carnegie held that a man ought to live modestly, provide for the legitimate needs of those who are dependent on him, and use his surplus in socially useful ways,

> the man of wealth thus becoming the mere agent and trustee for his poorer brethren, bringing to their service his superior wisdom,

experience, and ability to administer, doing for them better than they would or could do for themselves.[45]

Such an ethic of stewardship Carnegie greeted as the answer to economic inequity, and out of such stewardship he expected a social harmony that would replace class enmity. Poverty was understood in the gospel of wealth as ordinarily the result of immorality or lack of ambition, or occasionally of misfortune. So Carnegie exulted:

Avenues greater in number, wider in content, easier of access than ever before existed, stand open to the sober, frugal, energetic and able mechanic, to the scientifically educated youth, to the office boy and clerk — avenues through which they can reap greater successes than ever before within the reach of these classes in the history of the world.[46]

Poverty was, in fact, the demanding school out of which more than one millionaire had emerged, said the steel titan, and therefore the poor should be congratulated on the challenge that is theirs in hard work. " Such, in my opinion, is the true Gospel concerning Wealth, obedience to which is destined some day to solve the problem of the Rich and the Poor, and to bring ' Peace on earth, among men of good-will.' " [47]

This gospel was good news indeed to large numbers of Christians in the late nineteenth century who found in it a contemporary restatement of a traditional moralistic Protestant work ethic, combined with the appeal to individualism and charity which had been strong elements in revivalism. So Mark Hopkins wrote:

The acquisition of property is required by love, because it is a powerful means of benefitting others. . . . A selfish getting of property, though better than a selfish indolence or wastefulness, is not to be encouraged. . . . Industry, frugality, carefulness, as ministering to a cheerful giving, would then not only be purged from all taint of meanness, but would be ennobled.[48]

Russell Conwell, in his famous lecture "Acres of Diamonds," insisted that " to secure wealth is an honorable ambition, and is one test of a person's usefulness to others. . . . I say, Get rich, get rich! But get money honestly, or it will be a withering curse." [49] Bishop Lawrence of Massachusetts put the moral issue unequivocally: "In the long run, it is only to the man of morality that wealth comes. . . . Godliness is in league with riches." [50] The translation of this ethic into the popular cult of success is illustrated in William Makepeace Thackeray's *Tact, Push and Principle:* "Religion uses all the just motives of worldly wisdom, and adds thereto those higher motives that immortality creates. Indeed, we might say that religion demands success." [51]

Here, then, was an ethic that transcendentalized the prevailing economic mores, claiming for them the status of natural law and divine ordination, and which called upon men to accommodate themselves to those mores as an act of both patriotism and piety.

In sharp contrast, the transformationists insisted that faithfulness to the ethics of the New Testament would require a transvaluation of the prevailing cultural values, and most especially of industrial capitalism. This view is most commonly known as the social gospel. The transformationists themselves were divided over the ways in which the transvaluation was to take place, some insisting on the need for *social revolution,* and others holding out hope for its accomplishment by means of *social evolution.*

Walter Rauschenbusch was perhaps the chief spokesman for the advocates of social revolution — but it was to be a nonviolent revolution, since Rauschenbusch was persuaded that Jesus had repudiated violence as a means of establishing his Kingdom. Rauschenbusch was quite aware that Jesus was not a social reformer in the modern sense, since his approach to evil and suffering was moral rather than economic or historical. "He wanted men to live a right life in common, and only in so far as social questions are moral questions did he deal with them as they confronted him." [52] But Jesus was more than a teacher of morality. He had learned how to live the religious life, and it was this that he desired to impart to others. He knew that even when all economic questions are solved, the problems of human emptiness and meaninglessness may still haunt.

No comprehension of Jesus is even approximately true which fails to understand that the heart of his heart was religion. . . . But on the other hand no man shares his life with God whose religion does not flow out, naturally and without effort, into all relations of his life and reconstructs everything that it touches. Whoever uncouples the religious and the social life has not understood Jesus.[53]

The social nature of the religion of Jesus is to be seen, in Rauschenbusch's view, in the fact that the Kingdom of God was at the center of Jesus' teaching. In the New Testament,

the kingdom of God is still a collective conception, involving the whole social life of man. It is not a matter of saving atoms, but of saving the social organism. It is not a matter of getting individuals into heaven, but of transforming the life on earth into the harmony of heaven.[54]

To view the individual apart from society is a later heresy into which Jesus never fell.

The ethic of Jesus, then, is tied to the conception of the Kingdom of God as " humanity organized according to the will of God." " All human goodness is social goodness. . . . A man is moral when he is social; he is immoral when he is anti-social." [55] Sin is thus defined as selfishness, man's insistence upon living in a self-enclosed world and his repudiation of the human community in which God has placed him. Implied in this view is the social solidarity of mankind, in which the suffering and sin of one man entails the whole social organism. Sin and suffering are not vicarious, they are solidaristic. But if this solidarity serves to socialize suffering and evil, it serves equally to socialize the good and is thus the source of the greatest benefit to mankind. " It follows that ethically it is of the highest importance to prevent our beneficent solidarity from being twisted into a means of torture." [56]

Love is affirmed as the fundamental Christian ethical virtue, since love is the society-creating power. " In the measure in which love increases in any social organism, it will hold together without coercion." [57] Love means a determination that the fraternal relation that properly binds all men under God's Fatherhood shall not be ruptured. " This would be Christ's test for any custom, law, or institution: does it draw men together or divide them? " [58]

Taken with radical seriousness, Rauschenbusch was sure that the teaching of Jesus would result in a new social and political order. Between the genius of Christianity and the genius of capitalism, Rauschenbusch saw a " spiritual antagonism." " If we can trust the Bible, God is against capitalism, its methods, spirit, and results." [59] In *Christianizing the Social Order,* he provided a useful summary of the social gospel's critique of capitalism:

Religion declares the supreme value of life and personality, even the humblest; Business negatives that declaration of faith by setting up Profit as the supreme and engrossing object of thought and effort, and by sacrificing life to profit where necessary.

Christianity teaches the unity and solidarity of men; Capitalism reduces that teaching to a harmless expression of sentiment by splitting society into two antagonistic sections, unlike in their work, their income, their pleasures, and their point of view.

True Christianity wakens men to a sense of their worth, to love of freedom, and independence of action: Capitalism, based on the principle of autocracy, resents independence, suppresses the attempts of the working class to gain it, and deadens the awakening effect that goes out from Christianity.

The spirit of Christianity puts even men of unequal worth on a footing of equality by the knowledge of common sins and weakness, and by the faith in a common salvation; Capitalism creates an immense inequality between families, perpetuates it by property conditions, and makes it hard for high and low to have a realizing sense of equality which their religion teaches.

Christianity puts the obligation of love on the holiest basis and exerts its efforts to create fraternal feeling among men, and to restore it where broken: Capitalism has created world-wide unrest, jealousy, resentment, and bitterness, which choke Christian love like weeds.

Jesus bids us strive for the Reign of God and the justice of God, because on that spiritual basis all material wants too will be met: Capitalism urges us to strive first and last for our personal enrichment, and it formerly held out the hope that the selfishness of all would create the universal good.

Christianity makes the love of money the root of all evil, and demands the exclusion of the covetous and extortioners from the Christian fellowship: Capitalism cultivates the love of money for its own sake and gives its largest wealth to those who use monopoly for extortion.

Thus two spirits are wrestling for the mastery in modern life. . . . Each imposes its own laws and sets up its own God. If one is Christian, the other is unchristian.[60]

To those who urged men to get wealth honestly and to use it charitably, Rauschenbusch replied that it is impossible either to get great wealth or to give it away without creating mischief!

Rauschenbusch did not shrink from embracing the political movement of democratic socialism in practical support of his ethical program. Indeed, he declared that the social gospel "constitutes the moral power in the propaganda of socialism." [61] It is little wonder, then, that the social gospel of Walter Rauschenbusch was viewed by many with alarm as dangerously revolutionary.

Shailer Mathews was a leading representative of those within the social gospel movement who looked to evolution rather than to revolution in the transformation of culture. In *The Church and the Changing Order,* written in 1907, Mathews showed a marked uneasiness with the mood of social discontent that was upon the land. He feared that discontent in the areas of economics and politics and religion might spread to infect areas where it could serve no constructive purpose. The church should perform a moderating function in the midst of social unrest, contributing "the spirit of Jesus to the ideals which are provocative of discontent." [62] While he was persuaded that social problems must be remedied socially, he held that "in the long run, public opinion can be affected by modifying the sympathy and idealism of individuals." [63] The Sunday school could become an instrument in such a strategy of modification, Mathews thought, since it provides a means of contact with the workingman below the level of political and economic unrest. Regeneration of class consciousness is to be attempted " by the elevation and energizing of moral ideals of the representatives of both capital and labor." [64] While the pulpit should attack social abuses, its primary function should be directed toward creating moral sensitiveness. Since social privileges are largely in the hands of church members, the church should inspire Christians, as privileged members of society, to extend and share their privileges in the spirit of love and sacrifice. This would be " one of the most effective ways of allaying discontent and forestalling radicalism." [65]

Mathews did not trust the professional reformers of his time. " One real danger that threatens to-day's life," he wrote,

> is unemployed reformers. . . . Far be it from any one to disparage the motives of such enthusiasts, but . . . one cannot help seeing the danger that lies in unregulated and visionary amateur philanthropy. . . . Agitators are indispensable, but an agitator mad with altruism is as dangerous as any other madman.[66]

Anarchism and Christianity are totally incompatible, in Mathews' view, since it is better to obey bad laws than to repudiate all law. " Let reforms come; make reforms come; but let everything be done decently and in order." [67]

Mathews acknowledged the movement of democratic socialism as a child of the Christian church, but the difference between Christianity and socialism in his view was this: " Socialism assumes that the individual must be raised through his connection with a better social order; Christianity assumes that it is impossible to have a good social order composed of bad men." [68]

The church as an institution has no business in the movement of social reform.

> Reforms are for church members, not for churches. . . . A genuinely Christian church member is always material ready at hand for any rational social movement; and if a census were made of those who are effectively connected with social, municipal, and national reforms, it is no very rash statement that the large majority of such persons would be found to have come, either personally or through

family example, under the influence of some church. It should never be otherwise.[69]

Winthrop S. Hudson has provided a helpful summary of the differences of mood and method that divided Mathews and Rauschenbusch, fellow transformationists though they were:

Mathews was cautious, Rauschenbusch was impetuous. Mathews spoke of the necessity for adjustments and appropriations; Rauschenbusch spoke of the urgency for decisions. Mathews could look to the future with equanimity; Rauschenbusch was frequently beset with forebodings. Mathews believed in doing something *for* people; Rauschenbusch believed in doing something *with* people. Mathews placed his trust in middle class intelligence to effect social reform and thus remove the source of social discontent; Rauschenbusch believed in harnessing the discontent of the working-class to effect social reform. Mathews feared the word "socialism" because of its compulsive emotional power; Rauschenbusch cherished it for the same reason. Mathews believed that one of the most important functions of the church was "to keep social impulses law-abiding" and to "guarantee sanity in reform"; Rauschenbusch believed that a primary role of the church was to create a revolutionary ferment in society.[70]

These differences may be accounted for, at least in part, by the differences in background of the two men. Rauschenbusch began his professional career as a pastor in the Hell's Kitchen section of New York City, whereas Mathews began his career in the relatively detached world of education, briefly as an instructor at Newton Theological Institution and then as a teacher of history and political economy at Colby College. It may be important, in assessing their respective ideas about revolutionary social movements, to see that Rauschenbusch approached social protest from the experience of one who had tried to help socially disadvantaged men find some leverage against the forces that sought to perpetuate their disadvantage, whereas Mathews approached the problem of social unrest as an academic historian of the French Revolution. His book, *The French Revolution 1789–1815,* first appeared in 1900, and its usefulness was attested by the fact that it passed through four editions.

Rauschenbusch viewed the French Revolution as a force foı social good in spite of its lawlessness and destruction. In *Christianizing the Social Order,* he wrote that

every successful revolution unhorses privilege and flings open the door of opportunity to some new class that has hitherto been shut out, and this has sometimes set free such an opulence of intellectual ability and moral power that all the damage and disorder of a revolution were cheap. The French Revolution loosed an avalanche of ability and force over Europe.[71]

Historian Mathews was not so sure the matter was so unequivocal. While agreeing that the Revolution left a legacy of permanent good, he nevertheless took a much soberer view of it, and indeed found in it a vivid and persuasive historical example of the inability of revolution alone to achieve adequate social reform. In the end, said Mathews, it is social evolution that must confirm and extend and make permanent the gains to which the revolution is dedicated. The concluding paragraph of his history contains the moral that Mathews finds in his study of the revolution and enunciates the theme that subsequently appeared in *The Church and the Changing Order:*

All of these facts make it evident that revolutions are indications of the struggle for democratic rights. Political change and social evolution are more normal, but when the institutions of a country are outgrown and insufficient, when the creative ideals of a people are outraged by the selfish maintenance of monopolized privilege, revolution seems to be the inevitable last resort. Thus it is that although a comparison of the France of the Old Regime and the France of the Restoration does not disclose the realization of all the ideals for which the men of 1789 had hoped, it must be said that, despite the Terror and the distortion and perversion of French idealism by Napoleon's militarism, the Revolution brought to France and, through her expansion, to Europe permanent good. . . . And if all things had not become new in 1815, the promise of such creation had been given and partly fulfilled. *Social evolution had not been impotent and could not be crushed either by violence or radicalism or the forces of reaction. Therein lies the great meaning of the Revolution.* For if one has the eye to see the moral significance of this great period of social change, the failure of revolutionary violence and Napoleon's militarism to pass beyond the equality and rights gained by the French people through the voluntary surrender of privilege on August 4, 1789, makes it plain that *no reform can be permanent except that born of socialized ideals,* and that militarism, be it never so sagacious and efficient, is impotent to make a better world. *To give justice sacrificially is both nobler and wiser than to fight for the preservation of monopolized rights.*[72]

C. Institutionally, a distinction can be made among the liberals depending upon whether they were churchmen or nonchurchmen.

Probably no great number of liberals took up a deliberate position outside the institutional church. Much of the leadership for the liberal movement came from parish ministers. Still, a few of the academic theologians did their work from outside the organized church, and in this they anticipated the movement of theology out of the church that seems to be a characteristic of our own period.

At least two factors assisted the repudiation of institutional Christianity by the theologians. One was the influence of the German tradition of academic theology divorced from the life of the community of faith — a tradition that was imported into this country by American theological students returning from their pilgrimages to European centers of learning. The other was the indistinctness of the prevailing liberal view of the church. W. S. Hudson has described it as " the fading of any real distinction between the church and the world." Many liberals, says Hudson,

found it difficult to conceive of a church that did not embrace humanity indiscriminately. They had emphasized disposition and conduct as the essence of religion in order to ease their departure from the inherited faith and to facilitate the adjustment to a new set of theological convictions. But the new convictions did not provide any criteria for ethical discrimination, and consequently even at the point of conduct the possibility of a distinction between the church and the world was ruled out.[73]

This issue of churchmanship divided Shailer Mathews from his University of Chicago colleague George Burman Foster.

Mathews was himself an active and devoted churchman and served a term as president of the Northern Baptist Convention in 1915–1916, just eight years after its formation. Mathews the religious sociologist saw the crucial importance of the social and institutional vehicles that carry the permanent values of Christianity. In his autobiography, Mathews wrote that

> Professor Foster was a good representative of the movement in thought which was increasingly removed from the perception that Christianity is a religious movement rather than merely a system of truths. The importance of non-church-going religious philosophers is great but their influence is indirect if not negligible so far as operative Christianity is concerned. They find themselves increasingly out of sympathy with Christian groups and tend to dissociate themselves from organized religious work. The choice between such an attitude and that of a continued participation in organized church life sooner or later has to be made.[74]

The issue, however, was not forced during the period under study, even though there were a few defectors like Foster, and the liberal movement continued primarily within the institutional life of American Protestantism. One suspects that this was due less to theological or sociological conviction than to historical accident. In America, theology was predominantly church theology in the sense that most of the centers of professional theological activity, liberal or otherwise, had been founded by individual denominations and continued under their direct sponsorship. It is, therefore, scarcely surprising that the theological product of these schools assumed, where it did not specify, an institutional setting of the Christian life. Only later, when seminaries independent of any single institutional tradition came to dominate the theological enterprise, and when the call for a "religionless" Christianity reflected widespread disillusion with the unworldly irrelevance of the churches, did the anti-institutionalism, latent in this earlier liberalism, find popular articulation and support.

Five EPILOGUE: THE SHAPE OF THINGS TO COME

A. Recovery, or Return?

THERE IS PLENTY of evidence that a recovery of liberalism has been in the making for more than a decade. Some of that evidence was presented in the Prologue to this present work, and the work itself adds yet another item to the evidence.

A recovery of liberalism, however, is by no means the same thing as a return to liberalism, and it is important to make the distinction quite clear. This work of *recovery* is, in the first instance, historical, with theological criticism and construction built upon an objective restatement of the classic liberal credo. A *return* to liberalism would represent an attempt to make that credo normative again in the life of faith and the labor of the theologian. Since occasionally a call is heard for such a return, it is necessary in this Epilogue to go beyond restatement to an evaluation of the distinctive strengths and the besetting weaknesses of the movement. Unfortunately, such an evaluation must be based, in part, on evidence not presented in this book. Liberalism was by no means restricted to the eminent advocates whose views have been examined here, nor did it end where this present study ends. Liberalism became a popular movement in theology and its character partakes in part of that popular form.

Over a decade ago, a prominent liberal preacher-pastor issued a call for a return to liberalism.[1] Because his call was cast in the form that much popular liberalism came to take, and because it illustrates both the strengths and weaknesses to which the movement in general was heir, it provides a useful focus for critical evaluation. Alarmed by what seemed to him the unhealthy excesses of a prevailing neo-orthodoxy, he advocated "a theology of human relations that is psychologically and sociologically oriented." [2] He argued that when the contemporary insights of these social sciences "are joined in the religion of Jesus, we have a way of life that makes for wholeness." [3] It was precisely the fatal defect of neo-orthodoxy, in his view, that it had distorted and even perverted the religion of Jesus: (1) by emphasizing sin rather than salvation; (2) by its use of the doctrine of original sin as "a lazy substitute for what the love of Christ will do from the moment the baby is conceived"; (3) by an emphasis on man's limitations rather than his possibilities for growth; (4) by its preoccupation with man's guilt; and (5) by its view that salvation comes through the death of Jesus rather than by his life.[4] Such theology is irrelevant, because it ignores the basic insights of the natural and social sciences, of ethics and the arts, and it is demonic because it induces sickness in human life rather than exorcising it.[5]

Claiming Jesus as "my theologian" and the Sermon on the Mount as the source of "a theology of human relations," [6] this liberal preacher-pastor called for a faith at once relevant and healthy based on the following emphases in the teaching of Jesus: (1) the goodness of the child at birth; (2) the freedom of man to love and to be loved; (3) God as the indwelling spirit in man ("the real *you* is your link with God"); (4) Jesus, our elder brother and exemplar, whose spiritual and revelatory powers are not different in kind from those available to all men; and (5) life as a journey rather than a destination.[7]

If this interpretation of the teaching of Jesus and the task of theology illustrates some of the genuine strengths of the liberal tradition, it also demonstrates why no simple return to that tradition will do. Note, first of all, the liberal demand for a faith that is relevant to the human situation, both intellectual and interpersonal. Liberalism was, in fact, the first major tradition in the history of Christendom to make relevance a major intent of its theological program.

So it was one of the new notes, and permanent strengths, of the liberal tradition to declare that abstract or irrelevant theology is simply bad theology. Christian theology has two functions: to clarify the meaning of the gospel, and to mediate that meaning to the age. But no work of mediation can proceed in a vacuum. While this may appear an obvious point, it is one that circumstances in the recent history of theology require us to make clear. For one thing, there is the supposedly commonsense view, widely held by the laity and shared by not a few of the clergy, that the theologian and the theological enterprise lack practicality. It is too simple to write off this criticism as essentially anti-intellectual. Theology does stand under a certain obligation to practicality, if we understand that term to mean the fashioning of theological insight for the work of apologetic encounter and evangelism. It is the function of theology to be sensitive to men's questions in order that it may commend the answers which the gospel provides, and it is the function of theology, in sensitivity to the gospel, to commend to men the questions they ought to be asking.

Still another development that has encouraged the view of theology as an irrelevant exercise was the rise of fundamentalism in the 1920's and its resurgence in the post-World War II period. It has been the character of fundamentalism to defy the age rather than to seek to communicate with it, and if the neofundamentalists now declare their intention to reverse that situation, their continued polemics against evolutionary theory and social Christianity too regularly belie that intent. Theology has been taken traditionally by fundamentalism to have a narrow range of function, related almost exclusively to the salvation of the individual human soul in isolation from the social, economic, political, and intellectual environment. Fundamentalism, in the main, has not entered into active and open conversation with disciplines in the social, physical, and historical sciences, and has a seriously delimited theological ethic. On such terms, of course, theology is abstract, unrelated to real human conditions or questions, oblivious of the options that vie for men's spiritual allegiance.

Yet another development that has encouraged the notion of a theology independent of the age comes at nearly the opposite end of the theological spectrum, in what has been called the theological " positivism " of Karl Barth. Barthianism gives clear expression to a theology transfixed by a transcendent Word, which has nothing in common with our human words. Natural man has neither a capacity for nor a congeniality to the Word, and no human work can prepare him to receive it. Rather, the Word, in Barth's view, creates its own receptivity and casts its own illumination upon the human condition. Thus, theology is relieved of the necessity of attending to the demands of the time, or of inquiring into the questions men ask. It seeks self-consciously and assiduously to avoid expressing revelational ideas in terms of any " secular " ideology or idiom. Its task is solely that of proclaiming the Word as received.

But the Barthians needed to be reminded that the revelatory power of the Word depends, not simply upon some unique and *discontinuous* element which it thrusts freshly into the human situation, but precisely on its *continuity* with the human condition, which both precedes and follows it. The fact is that the Word comes to specific individuals, not in mystical transport out of the stream of concrete existence, but rather at particular junctures in personal and social existence. Thus, even the reception of the Word is itself conditioned by the internal and external history of those who receive it. It is, in fact, instructive to note how this European theological development was itself conditioned by a very concrete existential situation, growing as it did out of a reaction against a liberal theology that the clergy struggled to preach and their congregations struggled to receive in the wake of the First World War. Nor can the Word, in turn, be proclaimed, much less communicated, other than by the reconceptualization of what is received. Words and thought forms must be chosen that will at least be intelligible to those to whom the Word is proclaimed, and if the Barthian is not to fall into the fundamentalist error of mechanical dictation which he professes to abhor, he must allow that this process of reconceptualization is primarily a human activity.

Since, therefore, some relation will inevitably exist between theology and the age, the theologian is under obligation to seek deliberately and carefully to find the most faithful and fruitful relation. He can do this only by inquiring both into the insight that the Christian gospel gives concerning man's existence and into the questions men ask about themselves, the nature of their existence, the extent of their human powers, and the locus of their destiny. Attempt must be made by the theologian to enter sympathetically into man's actual aspirations and hopes, and appreciatively into his accomplishments. Only within the context of such inquiry can the whole theological task be accomplished, seeking both to apprehend the gospel and to mediate it to the age.

If the liberal was right in insisting on a relevant theology, he was clearly wrong in assuming that relevance required the surrender of theology to truth norms supplied by the secular intellectual disciplines. The preacher-pastor cited above is not untypical of the liberal's appeal to the natural and social sciences. In calling for " a theology of human relations that is psychologically and sociologically oriented," " a living theology illuminated by all the researches in the sciences," he was giving to the sciences a priority and an autonomy which he denied to the theological enterprise. It was, in fact, not clear from his call why we need theology at all. He seemed confident that the sciences themselves could supply the gospel, or at the very least, the sciences would provide the tests whereby the gospel, whatever its source, should be judged for its adequacy.

Such a view is scientifically deficient because it overlooks the tentative character of scientific insight, which is itself in need of continuous correction. One whole episode in American social history was unhappily written by those who assumed that the biological developmentalism discovered by Darwin could be directly applied to social institutions and that a steady transition from lower to higher in the organic scale was similarly the irreversible law of social growth. In *Contributions of Science to Religion,* Shailer Mathews supplied an unconscious but telling illustration of the peril involved even in seeking scientific analogies for theological truths. There Mathews wrote that the existence of God is as assured an inference of empirical science as is ether! [8]

For our purposes, it is not so much a distorted view of science as a distorted view of theology that is at issue in the liberal outlook. What seems totally absent is the very thing that is at the center of Biblical concern, namely, that theology depends first and last upon revelation. Theology, whatever else it may be, is primarily man's response to God's initiative in revealing himself, his nature, his purpose, his will. It is built upon the confession that God has been encountered, and it is the attempt to communicate that encounter in faithful and intelligible terms. This means that theology is not made up by pooling man's best insights about himself and the nature of the life he is called on to live, even when that pooling is derived with the care of scientific research. Revelation is received, not achieved, for the reason that the knowledge of God is a gift. First of all, it is given in the self-giving of God. Theology, therefore, has an integrity of its own quite apart from any other human discipline.

This is by no means to say that any particular theological system is self-evidently the right one, that any particular theological formulation has the character of a given. It is to say that every genuine theology is both created and judged by what is given — God in willing encounter with man.

A second liberal strength, found in the illustration with which this section began and pervasive of the whole movement, is the insistence that the general character of the religious dimension of experience is capable of yielding primary data for theology. In this, too, the liberals contributed something essentially new to the Christian theological enterprise. Before Schleiermacher in Germany, Coleridge in England, and Bushnell in

America, it would have seemed inappropriate to appeal, except secondarily, to the content of the religious consciousness for assured knowledge of God. If, prior to that time, there was an occasional pietist or mystic who dared to do theology in this way, the weight of tradition was against it; but Schleiermacher, Coleridge, and Bushnell shifted the traditional balance by conferring epistemological respectability on intuitive insight, thus enabling liberalism to become the first major theological movement to give so important a place to the witness of man's religious experience. Rudolf Otto's *The Idea of the Holy,* which first appeared in 1917, was perhaps the most eminent product of this new emphasis, and in its own right has been widely influential in establishing the permanent validity of the experiential mode.

Its validity lies in the fact that man exists at the juncture of the natural and the supernatural, as Bushnell argued. W. Paul Jones has preferred Immanuel Kant's terminology in making the same point. The religious question, in Jones's view, has to do with the " noumenal " dimension of all things: Is existence self-sustaining and self-explanatory, or is it God-contingent?

> Philosophers and scientists are beginning to see, rightly, that both logic and the scientific method are barred from answering this question. But if there is one case in which phenomenon and noumenon are identical, in which subject and object are one, then the chasm between knower and known that destroys certainty would be overcome. Only then would the truth about reality, the ultimate meaning, if any, be exposed.
>
> . . . It is obvious that a man can never become a tree or flower, can never know these from within, experience their noumenal essence, discover what it means for them to exist. . . . Such objects are destined to remain objects which confront man, always at a distance.
>
> What, however, about the case of the introspective self? Is this not the key for which we are looking? Here is the one case in which the subject, the apprehending self, is identical with that which is being apprehended, likewise the self. If man is ever to know the " really real," the " truly true," that innermost depth of reality that scientists such as Eddington clearly recognize but see as forever beyond

the grasp of scientific investigation, it will be in the process of the self introspecting profoundly the depths of its own existence.[9]

If, then, we are prepared to welcome the new liberal emphasis on human experience as datum for theology, we may not welcome the way in which the liberal enthusiasm for experience led to the virtual apotheosis of the behavioral sciences. " We need a theology of human relationships that is psychologically and sociologically oriented, a living theology illuminated by all of the researches in the sciences," wrote our liberal preacher-pastor. Since the preceding discussion of revelation bears directly on this point, it is necessary only to add a further comment. It is an easy step — and one which many liberals appeared to make — from calling for a " theology *of* human relations " to constructing theology *from* human relations. Biblically, and indeed by definition, theology is concerned primarily with the divine-human relationship, and then derivatively with human relationships. This clearly does not mean that human relationships are unimportant, and the " neighbor ethic " of the New Testament is only a single striking example of their importance. It does mean that human relationships are of a correlative importance derived from a prior datum that is given in man's encounter with that which both transcends and transforms even the most profound of human relationships.

A third strength to be noted lies in the value the liberals assigned, not simply to experience in general but specifically to the experiences of the Biblical men and women. Customarily, this meant the distinctively ethical experience that the Bible records, and appeal was most often made to the ethical proclamations of the Old Testament prophets and to the ethical teaching of Jesus, especially the Sermon on the Mount. Liberals never tired of pointing out that vital experience preceded and informed the written account in the Bible, that to value the writing over the experience was to do violence to the living truth of Biblical witness, and that the written word could become vital again only as it was translated into experiential terms. There can be little doubt that if the critical historical scholarship, which the liberals insisted on applying to the Biblical literature, occasionally resulted in skepticism concerning isolated aspects of the record, it more often restored to use large sections of the Bible that had become an embarrassment and that had fallen, therefore, into popular disuse or had been subjected to tortured and tortuous scholastic interpretation.

The error into which liberal historical scholarship fell, however, was the assumption of an oversimple identity between the historical experience of the nineteenth- or twentieth-century Biblical interpreter and the first-century Biblical witness, and therefore, an inability to permit to the Biblical period its own historical uniqueness. The result was that modern perceptions, essentially foreign and inaccessible to the Biblical men, were read into the Biblical record. In *The Quest of the Historical Jesus,* Albert Schweitzer showed how a developmental view, which depended upon evolutionary insight, had been made by nineteenth-century liberal scholarship to replace the cataclysmic eschatology of the first-century New Testament writers. It was said of Harnack, for example, that in his Biblical scholarship he was like a man looking into a deep well, who did not recognize that the image at the bottom was in fact a reflection of his own face.

This liberal error was not easily eliminated, in spite of the growing agreement of scholarly opinion since Schweitzer, and a popular liberalism has perpetuated the error. If one is to guess at the reason for this perpetuation, it may be a desire to give Biblical sanction to some of the preferred insights of contemporary psychology and sociology, or to give presumably scientific sanction to what are claimed to be the insights of Jesus. In either case, it is difficult to know where one would go in the teaching of Jesus to find such unqualified assertions as (1) that a child is born good, (2) that "the real *you* is your link with God," and (3) that the spiritual and revelatory powers of Jesus are not different in kind from those available to all men. It is not difficult, however, to know where one would go to find these or similar assertions in the work of some contemporary social scientists and popular writers.

Though the liberal claim that the New Testament is the source of its theological program was an appealing claim, one has the impression that in liberal hands the New Testament too frequently became a kind of casebook rich in material that illustrated some of the insights of the modern behavioral sciences. The result was to give those social scientific views a kind of ultimate significance which was, at the same time, effectively denied to the New Testament itself.

A fourth strength of liberalism lay in its emphasis on man's ability both to give and to receive love. If the liberals most often insisted that the complete fulfillment of love would depend finally on the intervening and infusing power of God's own love, they also felt free to insist that love is by no means totally foreign to man in his natural condition apart from special divine intervention. To be a man is to be morally free, and love is precisely the most distinctively human form man's freedom takes.

In this, too, the liberals were striking a largely new and somewhat daring note. Protestant orthodoxy had insisted on keeping man wholly in subjection to God, dependent for his saving good upon the special presence of the Holy Spirit in his life. Man over against God — not only in the sense of opposition to God, but simply standing on his own natural powers apart from God — was synonymous with sinful rebellion, in the orthodox view. Without yielding its evangelical allegiance, liberalism held that, if man is not able to complete his own life, he nevertheless has the ability to create and to fulfill proximate goods which will measurably affect his own spiritual good as well as the balance of good and evil in the world. Nor was the dignity conferred upon man by such freedom necessarily purchased at the expense of the divine dignity. On the contrary, orthodoxy had asserted that God holds all power, but it had never successfully dealt with the intellectual dilemma created by the fact that man patently exercises some power, and that the exercise of any power whatsoever other than God logically qualifies and limits God's power. Neither had orthodoxy successfully dealt with the corollary moral dilemma that results from asserting the absolute sovereignty of God while absolving him of all responsibility for evil. The orthodox had derogated God's dignity by perpetuating such unseemly and unnecessary dilemmas, in the liberal view. How much more clearly is the divine dignity served, and the sacrificial nature of the divine will revealed, by the recognition of a self-limiting God who loves his creatures too much to leave them powerless.

But enthusiasm for such a liberating and invigorating view of man's freedom to love led many liberals virtually to ignore man's tragically real experience of sin and guilt. Indeed, it was precisely the failure to take such experience seriously that made liberal theology irrelevant at a time when men were feeling the full and poignant weight of their culpability. The fact is that, if the sense of man's freedom and power is real in modern life, the sense of man's misuse of freedom and his consequent guilt is equally real, and not simply because the orthodox or the neo-orthodox have victimized men into believing in its reality. Said atomic physicist J. Robert Oppenheimer in reflecting on the first nuclear explosion: "In some sort of crude sense which no vulgarity, no humor, no overstatement can quite extinguish, the physicists have known sin: and this is a knowledge which they cannot lose." The atomic physicist is by no means the only one to experience the sharp ambiguity of contemporary life, at once creative and destructive. Ours is an age of ambiguity, and whoever would mediate the gospel to the age must be able to take sin and guilt seriously as constituting, at least in part, a real dimension of existence.

Surely the liberal is right in reminding us that a morbid preoccupation with sin and guilt to the exclusion of man's potent freedom is both theologically and personally unbalancing, and he is right in refusing to assign present responsibility for sin to some primordial event in the racial past. But today, no responsible Protestant theologian, and certainly no neo-orthodox theologian, blames a past event when he speaks of original sin. Rather, the Genesis myth is understood as illuminating an experience that is recapitulated in the life of every man. In the words of the late William Temple, it is that "each of us takes his place in the center of his own world. But I am not the center of the world . . . God is. In other words, from the beginning I put myself in God's place. This is my original sin." We might add, as indeed Dr. Temple did, that this process, contrary to the contention of our liberal preacher-pastor, takes place from birth. To blink that fact is to begin, not only theologically but psychologically, with a serious distortion of the human situation.

A fifth and intimately related strength lay in the conviction that society is capable of being ordered in terms of socialized love. The social gospel was one of the most distinctive and permanent contributions made to Christendom by the liberal movement. Never before had the structures of the common life been subjected to such systematic and searching Christian examination, and never before had the attempt been made to fashion the imperative of Christian love into concrete social and political programs in enthusiastic alliance with the growing forces of secular reform.

Social gospel liberalism held that society is not simply an aggregate of individuals to be affected only by first affecting its discrete individual members. The social organism is not the simple sum of its parts any more than the biological organism is, for when the parts are joined, its organic connections give it a distinctive power that could not have been guessed in examining the isolated parts, and a distinctive function that is more than the individual function raised to an aggregate power. Human society, in the liberal view, is one of the primary orders of God's creation and, as such, a direct object of God's redeeming concern.

If the liberals were thus able to make the sociopsychological distinction between individual man and society, they were less successful in distinguishing the ethical sanctions appropriate to each. To put the point even more accurately for some liberals, they failed to distinguish between man in his primary groups and man in his more impersonal conglomerates. The family thus became the model for society. In either case, it was assumed that since love is the sufficient norm for ordering the relations between man and man, it is also the sufficient norm for ordering the relations between man and his groups, as well as the relations among groups. It was the critical task of Reinhold Niebuhr in *Moral Man and Immoral Society* to show " the basic difference between the morality of individuals and the morality of collectives, whether races, classes or nations." [10] More specifically, Niebuhr wrote:

> Individual men may be moral in the sense that they are able to consider interests other than their own in determining problems of conduct, and are capable, on occasion, of preferring the advantages of others to their own. They are endowed by nature with a measure of sympathy and consideration for their kind, the breadth of which may be extended by an astute social pedagogy. Their rational faculty prompts them to a sense of justice which educational discipline may refine and purge of egoistic elements until they are able to view a social situation, in which their own interests are involved, with a fair measure of objectivity. But all these achievements are more difficult, if not impossible, for human societies and social groups. In every human group there is less reason to guide and to check impulse, less capacity for self-transcendence, less ability to comprehend the needs of others and therefore more unrestrained egoism than the individuals, who compose the group, reveal in their personal relationships.[11]

The liberal error lay in failing to place love in dialectic relation to justice in the development of a social ethic. Love demands that the good of each man be affirmed unconditionally; justice seeks to balance the competing goods of individual men and thus to create the greatest good for the greatest number. Love, apart from justice, may become irrelevant and, precisely because it cannot in practice affirm unconditionally the good of each man, may refuse to settle even for the limited goods that are within reach. Justice, apart from love, may become calculating and thus fail to serve the greatest number, because it loses sight of the greatest good. Love is justice seeking the largest good. Justice is love becoming relevant.

The sixth and final strength to be noted here is the liberal devotion to the historical person of Jesus. No earlier theological movement could have given so large a place to the human figure in the Gospels, because no earlier movement was the beneficiary of a historical science so advanced in the sophistication of its critical tools, the availability of its sources, and the actual scope of its historical knowledge. The liberals may, perhaps, be forgiven if they thought that God had reserved to such a time the privilege of taking the incarnation — the enfleshment of the transcendent Word — with a seriousness previously unmatched in Christian history. That is precisely what they intended to do, and their accomplishment cannot be gainsaid. Orthodox, and later neo-orthodox, theology was plagued by its inability to entertain the full incarnational reality, because it affirmed the Christ of faith to the virtual exclusion of the Jesus of history. If subsequent scholarship has shown that the liberals were sometimes mistaken in historical details and frequently overconfident in their expectations for the historical method, they nevertheless set the Man from Nazareth permanently in our midst. Not even a generation of neo-orthodox polemics has been able to displace the quest of the historical Jesus permanently, and if the " new quest " is more modest than the older liberal search, it nevertheless demonstrates again the liberal conviction that devotion to the historical Jesus is essential to the fullness of the gospel — indeed, that we have a gospel precisely because God cared enough about human life to share it.

Yet in another sense, liberalism typically dissipated the redemptive power of the incarnation by making it into a kind of moralistic principle. Wrote the liberal preacher-pastor cited earlier in this section:

> I believe that Jesus won a special relationship with God, and that he achieved a spiritual level where he had access to powers not ordinarily known. But did he have resources that are not available to us? Did God expect more of him than of every baby who is

born? . . . With resources available to you also he came to love as God loves, to feel as God feels, to live with God's wisdom and to know God's power. He became one with God. If you follow him with all your heart you will share his insight, tap his power, reveal God as he did.[12]

The understanding of salvation that emerges out of this purportedly " healthy " theology may be described, not unfairly, as a variety of the " do it yourself " activity so popular in our time. Men are called to become what they ought to become. In such a theology, man does not need a savior. He needs only a moral exemplar who will show him what the real possibilities of life are and will exhort him to their fulfillment.

Such a faith is simply inaccessible to many of our contemporaries. They do not lack ideals, either for themselves or for their world. They are not uncertain about what they want or what they ought to do. It is power they lack, not principle. In such a condition, no amount of exhortation to become what one ought to become will do. Indeed, it may increase the sense of immobility and deepen despair over it. So, ironically, the " healthy " theology may serve to complicate the disease. The interpretation of Jesus as the exemplar of the perfect life simply mocks men's longing for moral renovation, and there is no good news in that.

Liberal theology was right to reject the crude doctrines of the atonement that center upon the sacrificial death of Jesus as necessary to salvation. If an atoning death is one of the places in which the New Testament locates the power for new life, it is by no means the only place. Even more central to the whole of its witness is the confession that " God was in Christ reconciling the world to himself, not counting their trespasses against them." It is precisely this affirmation that any full and final understanding of incarnation and atonement must be able to take seriously. It suggests that God offers his acceptance to men, not because they merit it through moral achievement but because of his own active, seeking, restoring love. It says that human treachery, deceit, presumption, lust, impotence, have not the power to separate men from the forgiving love of God. It says that God did not wait until someone good enough came along to reveal this forgiving love, but that he took the initiative in man's redemption. It recognizes that no amount of striving could have purchased this redemption, separated as men are from God by the abyss which their own desire to play God has created. But it is God who has come over, restoring men to himself in the fellowship of Jesus Christ.

To call upon men to throw off sin and guilt in a vast effort to lift themselves by their own energy will not create power where none exists. To proclaim the active, seeking, restoring, enfolding, loving, forgiving acceptance of God may break through their isolation with a power which " makes all things new," renewing mind and will and heart and investing life with new meaning.

B. Current Themes in American Theology

It takes little daring, and even less prescience, to predict that, whatever form American theology takes in the next generation, it will not be a simple return to an earlier liberalism. Then what form will it take, and what influence will the current recovery of liberalism have in determining that form? It is much too early to answer either of those questions. Intellectual movements are notoriously difficult to detect in advance. Looking about, one discovers that they have, in fact, happened. Apparently promising ideas frequently fail to generate the necessary historical force to create a movement, while apparently insignificant intellectual developments may suddenly become the center of rapidly widening influence.

At the moment, American theology is in the backwash of neo-orthodoxy, having taken a small side excursion into creating a consensus theology in the service of ecumenical Christianity. If there is presently among us no new movement — the radical theology of the " death of God " can scarcely be described as a movement at this writing, and it is by no means certain to be as theologically important as its popular notoriety suggests — there are, nevertheless, strong currents out of which a future movement may come. Perhaps it is no accident that some of these currents stand in rather striking historical continuity with liberalism, and if it is not possible at the moment to draw the full significance from that connection, it will at least be important to note it.

In this section, then, we shall make only the briefest survey of some of these currents without attempting to evaluate them. They are drawn from the work of widely differing theologians, and no single theologian combines them all in a single system. Some of them will undoubtedly prove to be incompatible. These issues are receiving increasing attention, however, and may at least serve as pointers to the direction American theology is likely to take.

There is, first of all, a new demand for a theology that is relevant to a distinctively new human situation. Harvey Cox, of Harvard Divinity School, is probably the most influential voice here.

> The starting point for any theology of the church today [Cox writes] must be a theology of social change. The church is first of all a responding community, a people whose task it is to discern the action of God in the world and to join in His work. The action of God occurs through what theologians have sometimes called " historical events " but what might better be termed " social change." This means that the church must respond constantly to social change, but this is just the trouble. Our doctrines of the church have come to us from the frayed out period of classical Christendom and are infected with the ideology of preservation and permanence. They are almost entirely past-oriented, deriving their authority from one or another classical period, from an alleged resemblance to some earlier form of church life, or from a theory of historical continuity. But this will no longer do. A church whose life is defined and shaped by what God is *now* doing in the world cannot be imprisoned in such antiquated specifications. It must allow itself to be broken and reshaped continuously by God's continuous action; hence the need for a theology of social change.[13]

Cox may be described as the Rauschenbusch of the present theological generation, with the sudden impact of his first book *The Secular City* not unlike the impact of Rauschenbusch's first work *Christianity and the Social Crisis.* This is not to equate the points of view of the two men, but rather to suggest that each sharply and persuasively discerned the character of social revolution in his time, each sought a theology relevant to revolution, and each found in the Kingdom of God the appropriate symbol by means of which revolution and Christian response could be effectively and relevantly joined.

Secularization and urbanization describe what is distinctively new in the human situation, as Cox views it, and " the biblical image of the Kingdom of God " is to be " transcribed for our times into the symbol of the secular city, the commonwealth of maturity and interdependence." [14] To the objection that the Kingdom is God's work while the city is man's achievement, Cox replies that, " just as some theologians have interpreted the deity of Jesus as his readiness to accept and execute God's purpose for him, so the secular city signifies that point where man takes responsibility for directing the tumultuous tendencies of his time." [15] To the objection that the Kingdom demands renunciation and repentance while the secular city does not, Cox replies that " the Kingdom came in Jesus when God's doing something wholly new *coincided* with man's laying aside previous values and loyalties, and freely entering the new reality. Life in the emerging secular city entails precisely this kind of renunciation." [16] To the objection that the Kingdom is beyond history while the city is within it, Cox replies that New Testament scholarship has now moved beyond earlier debate between consistent and realized eschatology and speaks instead of " an eschatology which is *in process of realizing itself.* . . . If we accept this interpretation, then we live today in a world where what the New Testament writers described as the coming of the Kingdom *still* occurs." [17]

So a relevant Christian theology is one which discerns in the secular city the shape of God's work among us. " The Kingdom of God, concentrated in the life of Jesus of Nazareth, remains the fullest possible disclosure of the partnership of God and man in history. Our struggle for the shaping of the secular city represents the way we respond faithfully to this reality in our own times." [18]

Another way in which the contemporary demand for theological relevance is working itself out is to be found in the quest for a " religionless " interpretation of Christianity. Originally proposed by Dietrich Bonhoeffer in the literary fragments smuggled from his prison cell, this suggestion has widely caught the imagination of American seminarians and younger theologians. Bonhoeffer believed that for nineteen centuries, Christian preaching and theology has been based on the " religious premise " of man. Now it is becoming clear, he thought, that the religious was only a historically conditioned, temporary form of human behavior, and that contemporary man now lives "radically without religion." Thus the new problem for Christian preaching and theology can be stated this way: " How can Christ become the Lord even of those with no religion? " [19] Even more concretely, these questions emerge:

> What is the significance of a Church . . . in a religionless world? How do we speak of God without religion, i.e., without the temporally-influenced presuppositions of metaphysics, inwardness, and so on? . . . In what way are we in a religionless and secular sense Christians, . . . not conceiving of ourselves religiously as specially favoured, but as wholly belonging to the world? . . . What is the place of worship and prayer in an entire absence of religion? [20]

It is to this theological program that many American churchmen, inspired by Bonhoeffer's tantalizing but incomplete suggestions, are now addressing themselves.

A second theological current takes specific issue with Bonhoeffer and his followers, not at all on the demand for relevance, but specifically on the question whether man is to be understood as *homo religiosus*. Bonhoeffer, as we have already seen, believed that man's religious response to his existence was historically conditioned and had no ontological status in human nature itself. Barth held, somewhat differently, that the religious was the source of the idolatrous and that there was no way through from the religious to the Christian. Christianity, in

Barth's view, is not a religion but is precisely the abolition of religion.[21]

Recently, however, dissenting voices have begun to be heard. Richard R. Niebuhr, of Harvard Divinity School, has publicly confessed:

I do not understand the men who speak about religionless Christianity. I can understand a Christianity that is Protestant-less, bourgeois-less or Presbyterian-less. But the notion of a religionless faith strikes me as a doctrinaire tenet of a theology that has lost touch with human nature. For, I take it, no matter what else we may find it necessary to say about Christian faith, certainly experiencing such faith is a human act. And since man is undeniably a religious being I cannot make sense of those who separate religion and Christian faith. Such speculation seems to me as fanciful as the more familiar and traditional theorizing about man beyond all law.[22]

Similarly Langdon Gilkey, of the University of Chicago Divinity School, insists that " at his core man is a religious being, and this truth provides the clue both to his humanity and to his relation to God — for God-language is the explication of the answers to the deepest questions about man's existence." The " religious " character of man, in Gilkey's view, is seen in " the way in which his humaneness appears and is fed in those depths of his life where he finds himself related to an ultimate beyond himself." Modern man may interpret his experience in terms of secularity, says Gilkey, " but every action he makes in that world, every fear and anxiety he exhibits, and each deep joy he encounters there points to a dimension of his existence that transcends that narrow world." [23] Gilkey's colleague at Chicago, historian of religions Charles Long, holds that man is *homo religiosus* before he is *homo theologicus*. Beneath the problem of theology lies the problem of worship, " because in worship we see the expression of man's initial and primary contact with reality." The history of religions, says Long, describes the specific situation " in which man has given order to his world. It is the obligation of the sacred which expresses the ultimacy of man's being. The exploration of man's being and the discovery of new dimensions of reality are at the same time a confrontation with the sacred and ultimate reality." [24]

This recovery of a view of man as inherently religious provides an opening for the third theological current, which takes the form of renewed interest in human experience as a legitimate source of our knowledge of God. Langdon Gilkey puts the issue forthrightly:

> Our theological analysis must begin with man. If we felt sure that the divine word in Scripture was the truth, then the Bible might be our starting point. Or if we felt some assurance that existence as a whole was coherent, a metaphysical beginning might be possible. But in our situation these two certainties are lacking. What remains for us, as remained for Augustine and Schleiermacher in not unsimilar straits, is man as we can see him acting out his life around us, and as we feel the shape and depth of that human existence in ourselves.[25]

For a generation, the weight of Karl Barth's considerable theological authority stood opposed to this current, and Barth's strictures against Schleiermacher, the theologian of the distinctive religious consciousness, were widely accepted. Barth wrote that in Schleiermacher's work, " it is not the Holy Spirit, but as Schleiermacher claims, merely man's religious consciousness which has after all become the theme of his theology." In equating the divine Word with the form of " that which is historically effective and original," said Barth, Schleiermacher was able to do justice to modern cultural consciousness, " but possibly not to Christianity." [26] If Van Harvey is right, however, Barth's continuing preoccupation with Schleiermacher had ironic effect. Harvey has commented that " Barth taught us to read 19th century theology so that we might be immunized against its seductions. In reading it, we wondered whether Barth had read it correctly and whether it did not have something to say to us and to our situation." [27]

Harvey, of Southern Methodist University School of Theology, found himself attracted again to Schleiermacher's theological program: the attempt " to point to the crucial difference between the immediate utterances of the religious self-consciousness — which have, so to speak, their own logic — and the more abstract philosophical attempts to extend, relate and systematize the truth claims implicit in faith." [28] Harvey holds that the symbols employed in religious discourse " are ways of envisaging certain basic elements in our experience and that they make sense not as objects of belief but as images rooted in certain basic parables that illumine our ordinary human experience." [29]

Richard R. Niebuhr, in introducing a series of public lectures at Cambridge University on the religious affections, commented that he had been inoculated with Barth and had had a small infection followed by a violent reaction against the speculative character of Barth's theology. So Niebuhr has determined to approach theology once again from the point of view of human experience. Protestant academic theology, Niebuhr wrote in another context,

> has too long suffered an irrational fear of anthropocentrism. We have supposed that all our theological thinking must begin with God, because God is " that than which no greater can be conceived." And so we do believe. But theology is not bound to the order of being, nor is its chief business to protect God's firstness in this order. Indeed, part of its business is to explore the consequences of the peculiar way in which our knowledge of God has become ours.[30]

So theology, as Niebuhr understands it, is " a human endeavor that draws life from the primary, complex utterances of *human* faith," and faith is " the disposition that arises out of and is called forth from the compounded fears, passions, beliefs, hopes and other materials of human religion." So, " the renewal of theological energy can come only when we are willing to immerse ourselves again in the actual world where religion and faith live." [31]

Fresh interest in natural theology is a fourth and somewhat related current. Barthianism, on the one hand, and existentialism, on the other, have fed a predominantly antimetaphysical mood in theology in the recent past. Schubert Ogden, of Southern Methodist University School of Theology, agrees that it is necessary to break the hold of classical metaphysics upon Christian theology, since " God as traditionally conceived — as wholly absolute and unchanging Being — is actually the negation of the secular order in its autonomy and significance." [32] But if *secularism* is inherently antimetaphysical as it is inherently anti-Christian, *secularity* is not, and Ogden thinks the distinction is a crucial one. Furthermore, the claim to truth made by Christian faith inevitably entails metaphysical considerations. The Christian claim to truth can only be supported " if the critical reflection on our experience by science and philosophy does not rule out but requires two basic affirmations: first, of our own existence as free and responsible persons; and, second, of the existence of God as the eminently personal ground both of ourselves and of the world." [33] There is simply no way for theology to avoid meeting these two essentially philosophical conditions. " If we can be theologians today only by restricting our assertions to what is warrantable by the sciences and by being in no sense ' metaphysical ' or ' theistic,' then I would think the more honest way to say this is that we cannot be theologians today at all." So Ogden concludes that, " while in many ways I feel close to those of my contemporaries who are seeking a ' nonreligious interpretation of biblical concepts,' or the ' secular meaning of the gospel,' I cannot join them in their massive antimetaphysical demands." [34]

Van Harvey shares the view that religious truth claims are bound up with the truth claims of ontology. " By ontology," says Harvey, " I mean not the construction of a world behind the world but the systematic description of the structures of existence as they are implicitly affirmed in certain basic forms of human thought and action." [35] Harvey holds that the traditional separation of general revelation (which is the realm of natural or philosophical theology) from special revelation is a false dichotomy. The latter requires the former.

The reason a historical event grasps us as revelatory is that it throws into relief certain deep and elemental facts. Its power consists in its fusion of particularity and universality. The event of Jesus Christ is a revelation just because it poses in a decisive way the basic question of the logos, the inner structure of things.[36]

Langdon Gilkey, in calling for " drastic " theological reconstruction, explicitly denies that this must take the form of a new natural theology. In spite of that denial, however, Gilkey asserts the availability — and indeed the theological necessity — of a knowledge of God independent of special revelation, which is precisely the traditional premise of natural theology. So he insists that, " however God may be known, the knowledge of his reality is logically prior to all else; no revelation, no Christ of faith, no ecclesiology is ultimately possible or intelligible if the category of deity remains totally empty." [37]

Fresh interest in natural theology is bringing with it renewed interest in the philosophy of Alfred North Whitehead, called by John Cobb, of Southern California School of Theology, " the most comprehensively adequate synthesis of scientific and humanistic thought available," whose " congeniality to Christian faith should give us great joy." [38] Schubert Ogden also notes that " Whitehead has secured the foundations of a general metaphysical position which is a distinct alternative to all the classical systems but which . . . easily rivals them in scope as well as depth." Ogden also pays tribute to Charles Hartshorne, who " has succeeded in working out a neoclassical conception of God which not only is capable of meeting the usual objections to traditional theism " but may also succeed in reversing Pascal's famous dictum that the God of Abraham, Isaac, and Jacob is *not* the God of the philosophers.[39]

A fifth current is to be found in a new mood of optimism among some theologians. William H. Hamilton, of Colgate Rochester Divinity School, one of its leading spokesmen, writes that " optimism is a possibility for many and a necessity for some today in a way that has not been the case in America for some time." By optimism, Hamilton means " an increased sense of the possibilities of human action, human happiness, human decency, in this life." [40] Neo-orthodoxy, in reaction against the earlier liberal optimism, created a popular pessimism marked by a sharp awareness of man's limitations and of the tragic sense of life. But neo-orthodoxy is in theological trouble these days, Hamilton observes, and " I suspect that one of the reasons why neo-orthodoxy now doesn't work is that this pessimism doesn't persuade any more." [41] A new and more optimistic mood can be seen in many areas of human activity. In the social sciences, for example, a Lewis Mumford, who " understood, but did not enjoy, the world the machine brought," is giving way to a Marshall McLuhan or a Kenneth Boulding, who " understands, delights in, and invites all men to delight in the new media of the post-civilized world." [42] The notion of art as " the imposition of the artist's selfhood and creativity on the chaos of experience " is giving way to the notion that " the end of artistic creativity is not order or value but purposeless play, a play that affirms life and invites other men to wake up to the ordinary life around them that can be lived here and now." [43] In the civil rights movement, " there is a gaiety, an absence of alienation, a vigorous and contagious hope at the center," and " this optimism is the main source of its hold on the conscience of America." [44] If one seeks for theological factors that support the new optimism, Hamilton is inclined to locate them in the radical new " theology of the death of God." Tragedy is generated in the dialectic between the presence and the absence of God — when God is remembered, the world is forgotten and devalued, and when God is forgotten, the world is remembered and valued. As long as God lives, man " can never really love or care for anything in the world, but can only feel longing and incompleteness in it." [45] Now, however, the dialectic between presence and absence has been broken, in Hamilton's view: " Absence has won a decisive victory over the presence," [46] leaving tragedy a theological impossibility.

This is not an optimism of grace, but a worldly optimism I am defending. It faces despair not with the conviction that out of it God can bring hope, but with the conviction that the human conditions that created it can be overcome, whether those conditions be poverty, discrimination, or mental illness. It faces death not with the hope for immortality, but with the human confidence that man may befriend death and live with it as a possibility always alongside.

I think that the new optimism is both a cause and a consequence of the basic theological experience which we today call the death of God.[47]

But the new optimism is by no means limited to those who share Hamilton's radical theological disposition. Harvey Cox, for example, responds sharply that, "contrary to the seminary obituary columns, it is theology, not You Know Who, that is dead."[48] Yet, we have already noted Cox's optimistic enthusiasm for the twin revolutions of secularization and urbanization, which are creating a new environment for human life. Secularization "removes adolescent illusions. Freed from these fantasies man is expected to assume the status of sonship, maturity, and responsible stewardship."[49] Urbanization is the human effort to formulate "ways to live more equably with other human beings in a system of increasing reciprocity."[50] Together, says Cox, they disclose the lineaments of the Kingdom of God. Earlier, Gibson Winter, of the University of Chicago Divinity School, had expressed a similar optimism:

Metropolis is the form of the new society; it is emerging out of a welter of conflicting interests. Metropolis is the possibility of a unified, human society arising from the chaos of our massive, urbanized areas. Metropolis is the mother city, the nurturing totality of interdependent regions and municipalities where children may find a climate conducive to growth, where education may enrich life as well as capacities, where men and women may have opportunity to participate as members and receive their rewards, and where advantages may be distributed with equity. Metropolis is the realization of unity of life out of conflicting factions which now plague metropolitan areas. Metropolis is the fulfillment of the oneness of mankind out of the division of races and classes that now disrupts the metropolitan areas of our country. Metropolis is the human society which different groups subvert and which all groups need for their well-being. Metropolis is the power of the New Mankind refracted through human history.[51]

Closely related to the new optimism is a sixth current that places fresh emphasis on love as the sole and sufficient norm of ethical behavior.

One of the forms this emphasis takes is the " new morality " that was popularized in Bishop John A. T. Robinson's *Honest to God*. Bishop Robinson understands love as " unreserved self-giving." It does not bring fixed moral precepts to the ethical situation. Rather, it seeks to be responsive, in the midst of the concrete ethical situation, to the fullest range of possibilities for achieving the good.

> Love alone, because, as it were, it has a built-in moral compass, enabling it to " home " intuitively upon the deepest need of the other, can allow itself to be directed completely by the situation. It alone can afford to be utterly open to the situation, or rather to the person in the situation, uniquely and for his own sake, without losing its direction or unconditionality. It is able to embrace an ethic of radical responsiveness, meeting every situation on its own merits, with no prescriptive laws.[52]

Reinhold Niebuhr had earlier leveled his not inconsiderable critical guns at the love ethic of liberalism, declaring love to be an " impossible possibility " because " the collective behavior of mankind is not imaginative enough to assure more than minimal approximations of the ideal." [53] This did not mean, for Niebuhr, that love was irrelevant to the ethical situation; it meant, rather, that its relevance is not as a quality to be achieved but as a critical principle against which to judge the approximations of justice. Joseph Fletcher, of the Episcopal Theological School, who has given the situational ethic of the " new morality " a thorough and systematic statement, replies that Niebuhr's error lay in thinking of love as an absolute property or state, " as something we *have* in one measure or another."

> But love is not something we *have* or *are,* it is something we *do*. Our task is to act so that more good (i.e., loving-kindness) will occur than any possible alternatives; we are to be " optimific," to seek an optimum of loving-kindness. It is an attitude, a disposition, a leaning, a preference, a purpose. . . . We cannot therefore speak with

Niebuhr of the "impossibility" of love, even though we join him in speaking of its *relativity*. Love does not say to us, "*Be* like me." It says, "*Do* what you can where you are." [54]

The ethical task, for Fletcher, is "to find absolute love's relative course." "What is to be done in any situation depends on the case, and the solution of any moral issue is, therefore, quite relative. . . . But once the relative course is chosen, the obligation to pursue it is absolute. . . . Only the *how* is relative, not the *why*." [55]

But if Fletcher and his fellow situational ethicists are content to insist that love is always a predicate and never a substantive, other Christians in these days have been giving courageous witness to a substantive view of love as nonviolent resistance. Pacifism, which came to be one of the hallmarks of the liberal social gospel, was rejected by neo-orthodoxy as an ineffective and irrelevant instrument of social policy in conflict situations, but it has now reemerged in the nonviolent demonstrations of the civil rights movement. If the success of the nonviolent techniques of Martin Luther King are difficult to assess in such a seething situation, and if they are now being challenged from within the civil rights movement by its more impatient and belligerent elements, their success has, nevertheless, been sufficient to generate a growing serious and sympathetic reappraisal of the pacifist philosophy and a new determination to translate Christian love into a nonviolent strategy aimed at the current deadlock, or balance of terror, in international politics.

The final current is Christological, and it involves a reaffirmation of the Lordship of Jesus and a call to discipleship in his cause. It is not as surprising as it might seem, at first, that this double theme is being expressed with considerable vigor by the radical theologians of the "death of God." Dietrich Bonhoeffer, one of the sources of the radical theology, had written that Jesus Christ, no longer an object of religion, is now free to be the Lord of the whole world, and Christian discipleship is, therefore, fulfilled in willingness to participate with God in the suffering of the world. William Hamilton, boldly affirming God's demise, asks what is to be put in God's place. One answer is, "the human community," which must now learn how to do what once God did — forgive with radical and unconditioned grace, comfort and console, judge, check, rebuke.

But it would be misleading to pass over to what we are calling the human community every task once given to God. . . . If by God you mean the focus for obedience, the object of trust and loyalty, the meaning I give to love, my center, my meaning — then these meanings are given not to men in general but to Jesus, the *man,* in his life, his way with others and his death. We death-of-God theologians thus stake out a claim to be able to make it as Christians . . . because we see as the center of Christian faith a relation of obedience and trust directed to Jesus.[56]

There is evident in Hamilton a kind of secular neo-Ritschlianism. Ritschl had insisted that the Christian does not have an objectively validated idea of God prior to the appearance of Jesus, against which the divinity of Jesus is measured and confirmed; rather, Jesus supplies the normative content of divinity in the event of his appearing. Similarly for Hamilton, to ask, "Do you believe in the divinity of Christ?" assumes that there are two known categories — divinity, and Jesus the man.

But the point is this: we do not have two known categories at all. We have Jesus the man. Of him we know something; not enough to satisfy, not enough to provide answers to our ethical problems, but enough to be able to say what was characteristic of him and his way with men. And we have further a decision of faith that Jesus is the Lord, the one through whom God meets us. . . . "In Jesus the Lord, the whole meaning of what it is to be God is so radically transformed that we can no longer move from divinity to Jesus . . . but from Jesus to divinity. . . ." [57]

If one asks what this new content of divinity is, Hamilton replies that "it is God withdrawing from all claims to power and authority and sovereignty, and consenting to become himself the victim and subject of all the world can do. . . . Divinity in Jesus is not withdrawal from the world; it is a full consent to abide in the world, and to allow the world to have its way with it." [58]

The Christology of the radical theologians stands out with a special clarity — and creates special problems as well — because it is not supported by the full apparatus of Christian doctrine. However, it is precisely the Christological demand made by other aspects of Christian doctrine, as they are fashioned into a theology of social change, which has led Harvey Cox to a fresh appreciation of the importance of Jesus. If Christians are ever to give up thinking " religiously " and begin to think both theologically and politically, says Cox, it will require a recovery of " the gritty historicity of Israel's faith," and this will mean repairing the breach between the Old and New Testaments.

> The link between the church and Israel is Jesus of Nazareth, and the fault for making him more of a barrier than a bridge lies mainly on the Christian side. We need as our theological starting point a Jesus who is neither the ecclesiastical nor the existentialist Jesus, but the Jewish Jesus. Not the Jesus toward whom the church has developed a downright proprietary attitude, but the Jesus who destroys the temple. Our Christology must begin with the Jew who makes it possible for us to share the hope of Israel, the hope for a Kingdom of Shalom.[59]

But Cox is persuaded that our theology will continue to be abstract and thus inadequate unless it emerges out of our obedience; that Christology requires discipleship. " Does it seem too obsolete," Cox asks,

> to suggest that even for theologians " following Jesus " is a necessary prerequisite to right *thinking* about him? Or that "following Jesus " will inevitably make us participants and not just onlookers in today's social revolution? Theology detached from discipleship, theology outside the prophetic fellowship, becomes barren. To follow Jesus means to be on the move, to abandon old formulations when they no longer serve, to address new issues as they appear.[60]

" Following Jesus " is similarly the concern of Langdon Gilkey, for it is discipleship which puts man in touch with what it is authentically to be a man. Gilkey writes:

> The freedom of Jesus from self and for others, the compassion and concern he felt and enacted for our human needs, come to us as the authenticated pattern for our own humanity, as the form in which the ultimate which is our origin claims us for itself. And we know

that in these terms alone can we find our true selves. . . . In this sense he is our " Lord," who provides us with our ethical model or perspective.[61]

Discipleship may also be the key to the solution of another vexing theological problem, that of giving vital content to our God-language. For Gilkey is convinced that

when we thus begin with an experience of what has been called " the benefits of Jesus," that as we explore this relation to him, we shall find that we must speak of more than Jesus himself — we must begin as well to use God-language. For in so far as he has this relation to us, only through him can the claim, the judgment and the saving power of *God* be mediated to our present life. Some power that transcends his passing and continues as the ground of our own fleeting present must come to us through this strange and lordly figure of the past who so vividly calls us and so directly transforms our being — for no dead human being from the vanished past could so compel and rescue us in the living present.[62]

C. Conclusion

If it is too early to mark in detail the direction American theology will take in the next generation, the evidence of this present chapter does seem to support an observation and a prediction.

The observation is that the mood which is now growing up can be called " liberal " without doing violence either to the classical liberalism described in Chapters Three and Four or to the analysis given in this Epilogue. There is clearly a new respect for the way the older liberals did theology — for the questions they asked, for the methods they employed, and for the sources they probed — and a new willingness to explore the possibility of doing theology that way in our own generation.

The prediction is that the result will be a mediating theology, just as liberalism in its own time was a mediating theology. The peculiar program of the contemporary theologian is to work out a new Christian faithfulness in the presence of the demands made by the systematic theology of a Barth and a Tillich, the ontology of a Heidegger and a Whitehead, the social policy of a Reinhold

Niebuhr and a Martin Luther King, the intellectual insights of the nineteenth century, and the cultural needs of the twentieth.

Insofar, it will be a period of theological instability, for as H. Richard Niebuhr has remarked, "No mediating theology in history has ever been able to keep in balance the opposing elements it seeks to reconcile." [63]

If the prospect is thus for an absence of the synoptic vision and an unlikelihood of theological system-building on the classical models, it nevertheless promises an exciting series of theological engagements whose very particularity will make them all the more intense, and whose consequent energy will make possible a faithful response to the movement of God in the history of our own time.

APPENDIX: BIOGRAPHICAL NOTES[1]

The following biographical data are supplied as a supplement to Chapters Three and Four. Publications listed are representative rather than exhaustive, and usually only those works are cited which appeared during the period of this study (1879–1917).

Abbott, Lyman. Congregationalist. B. Roxbury, Mass., December 18, 1835; d. October 22, 1922. Graduated, New York University, 1853. Practiced law, 1853–59; pastor, Terre Haute, Ind., 1860–65; secretary, American Union (Freedmen's) Committee, 1865–68; pastor, New England Church, New York City, 1866–69; editor, *The Illustrated Weekly,* 1870–76; *The Christian Union* (later *Outlook*), 1876–1922; pastor, Plymouth Church, Brooklyn, 1890–99. *The Evolution of Christianity* (1892); *The Theology of an Evolutionist* (1897); *The Life and Literature of the Ancient Hebrews* (1901); *Henry Ward Beecher* (1903).

Beecher, Henry Ward. Congregationalist. B. Litchfield, Conn., June 24, 1813; d. March 8, 1887. Graduated, Amherst College, 1834; Lane Theological Seminary, Cincinnati, 1837. Pastor, Presbyterian Church, Lawrenceburg, Ind. 1837–39; Indianapolis, 1839–47; Plymouth Church, Brooklyn, 1847–87; editor, *The Independent,* 1861–64; *The Christian Union,* 1870–81. *Seven Lectures to Young Men* (1844); *Yale Lectures on Preaching* (1872–74); *Evolution and Religion* (1885); *The Life of Jesus Christ* (Vol. I, 1871; Vol. II, posthumous, 1891).

Brown, William Adams. Presbyterian. B. New York City, December 29, 1865; d. December 15, 1943. B.A., Yale, 1886; M.A., 1888; Ph.D., 1901; graduated, Union Theological Seminary, 1890; studied in Berlin, 1890–92. Taught church history and systematic theology, Union Theological Seminary, 1893–1936; Roosevelt professor, 1898–1930. *Christ the Vitalizing Principle of Christian Theology* (1898); *The Essence of Christianity*

(1902); *Christian Theology in Outline* (1906).

Case, Shirley Jackson. Baptist. B. Hatfield Point, New Brunswick, September 28, 1872; d. December 5, 1947. B.A., Acadia University, 1893; M.A., 1896; B.D., Yale, 1904; Ph.D., 1906; University of Marburg, 1910. Taught mathematics and Greek in preparatory schools, 1893–1901; New Testament Greek, Yale, 1905–06; history and philosophy of religion, Bates College, 1906–08; New Testament interpretation and early church history, University of Chicago, 1908–38; dean, University of Chicago Divinity School, 1933–38. *The Historicity of Jesus* (1912); *The Evolution of Early Christianity* (1914).

Clarke, William Newton. Baptist. B. Cazenovia, N.Y., December 2, 1841; d. 1912. B.A., Madison (now Colgate) University, 1861, M.A., 1863; graduated, Hamilton Theological Seminary, 1863. Pastor, Keene, N.H., 1863–69; Newton Center, Mass., 1869–80; Montreal, Canada, 1880–83; taught New Testament interpretation, Toronto Baptist College, 1883–87; pastor, Hamilton, N.Y., 1887–90; taught Christian theology, ethics, and apologetics, Colgate University, 1890–1912. *Outline of Christian Theology* (1898); *What Shall We Think of Christianity?* (1899); *The Use of the Scriptures in Theology* (1905); *Sixty Years with the Bible* (1909).

Conwell, Russell Herman. Baptist. B. Worthington, Mass., February 15, 1843; d. December 6, 1925. Studies at Yale Law School interrupted by service as Civil War infantry officer; LL.B., Albany Law School, 1866. Practiced law, Minneapolis, 1865–67; immigration agent from Minnesota to Germany, 1867–68; foreign correspondent, New York *Tribune* and Boston *Traveler,* 1868–71; practiced law, Boston, 1871–79; pastor, Grace Baptist Church, Philadelphia, 1881–91; Baptist Temple, Philadelphia, 1891–1925; founded Temple College (now University), 1888, and was its first president. *Acres of Diamonds;* biographies of Rutherford Hayes, James A. Garfield, James G. Blaine, and Charles Spurgeon.

Fosdick, Harry Emerson. Baptist. B. Buffalo, N.Y., May 24, 1878. B.A., Colgate University, 1900; B.D., Union Theological Seminary, 1904; M.A., Columbia University, 1908. Pastor, First Baptist Church, Montclair, N.J., 1904–15; First Presbyterian Church, New York City, 1919–25; Park Avenue Baptist Church (later Riverside Church), 1925–46; taught homiletics and practical theology, Union Theological Seminary, 1908–46. *The Manhood of the Master* (1913); *The Assurance of Immortality* (1913); *The Meaning of Prayer* (1915); *The Meaning of Faith* (1917).

Foster, George Burman. Baptist. B. Alderson, W. Va., April 2, 1858; d. December 22, 1918. B. A., West Virginia University, 1883; M.A., 1884; graduated, Rochester Theological Seminary, 1887; studied at Göttingen and Berlin, 1891–92. Pastor, Saratoga Springs, N.Y., 1887–91; taught philosophy, McMaster University, 1892–95; systematic theology and philosophy of religion, University of Chicago, 1895–1918. *The Finality of the Christian Religion* (1909); *The Function of Religion in Man's Struggle for Existence* (1909); *The Function of Death in Human Experience* (1919).

Gladden, Washington. Congregationalist. B. Pottsgrove, Pa., February 11, 1836; d. July 2, 1918. B.A., Williams College, 1859. Pastor, Brooklyn, 1860–61; Morrisiana, N.Y., 1861–66; North Adams, Mass., 1866–71; editorial staff, New York *Independent,* 1871–74; pastor, Springfield, Mass., 1875–82; editor, *Sunday Afternoon,* 1878–80; pastor, Columbus, Ohio, 1882–1914. *Plain Thoughts on the Art of Living* (1868); *Workingmen and Their Employers* (1876); *Things New and Old* (1884); *Applied Christianity* (1886); *Present Day Theology* (1913).

Gordon, George Angier. Congregationalist. B. Oyne, Aberdeenshire, January 2, 1853; d. October 25, 1929. Graduated, Bangor Theological Seminary, 1877; B.A., Harvard, 1881. Pastor, Temple, Maine, 1877–78; Greenwich, Conn., 1881–83; Old South Church, Boston, 1884–1927. *The Christ of Today* (1895); *New Epoch for Faith* (1901); *Ultimate Conceptions of Faith* (1903).

Hillis, Newell Dwight. Congregationalist. B. Magnolia, Iowa, September 2, 1858; d. February 25, 1929. B.A., Lake Forest University, later M.A.; graduated, McCormick Theological Seminary, 1887. Pastor, First Presbyterian Church, Peoria, Ill., 1886–89; Evanston, Ill., 1889–94; Central Church (independent), Chicago, 1895–99; Plymouth Church, Brooklyn, 1899–1924. *A Man's Value to Society* (1896); *The Investment of Influence* (1898); *The Influence of Christ in Modern Life* (1900); *The Fortune of the Republic* (1906).

Macintosh, Douglas Clyde. Baptist. B. Breadalbane, Ontario, February 18, 1877; d. July 6, 1948. B.A., McMaster University, 1903; Ph.D., Chicago, 1909. Pastor, Baptist Church, Marthaville, Ontario, 1897–99; taught philosophy, McMaster, 1903–04; Biblical and systematic theology, Brandon (Manitoba) College, 1907–09; systematic theology and philosophy of religion, Yale, 1909–42; Dwight professor, 1916–32. *The Reaction Against Metaphysics in Theology* (1911); *The Problem of Knowledge* (1915); *Theology as an Empirical Science* (1919).

Mathews, Shailer. Baptist. B. Portland, Maine, May 26, 1863; d. October 23, 1941. B.A., Colby University, 1884; M.A., 1887; graduated, Newton Theological Institution, 1887; studied in Berlin, 1890–91. Taught rhetoric, Colby, 1887–89; history and political economy, 1889–94; New Testament literature, Newton Theological Institution, 1888–90; New Testament history and interpretation, systematic theology, University of Chicago, 1894–1933; dean, University of Chicago Divinity School, 1908–33. *The Social Teaching of Jesus* (1897); *A History of New Testament Times in Palestine* (1899); *The French Revolution* (1900); *The Church and the Changing Order* (1907); *The Social Gospel* (1909), *The Spiritual Interpretation of History* (1916).

Munger, Theodore Thornton. Congregationalist. B. Bainbridge, N.Y., March 5, 1830; d. 1910. Graduated, Yale College, 1851; Yale Divinity School, 1855. Pastor, Dorchester, Mass., 1856–60; Haverhill, Mass., 1862–70; Lawrence, Mass., 1870–75; San Jose, Calif., 1875–76; North Adams, Mass., 1876–85; United Church, New Haven, Conn., 1885–91. *On the Threshold* (1881); *The Freedom of Faith* (1883); *Horace Bushnell, Preacher and Theologian* (1899).

Rauschenbusch, Walter. Baptist. B. Rochester, N.Y., October 4, 1861; d. July 25, 1918. B.A., University of Rochester, 1884; graduated, Rochester Theological Seminary, 1886; studied in Germany, 1891–92, 1907–08. Pastor, Second German Baptist Church, New York City, 1886–97; taught New Testament interpretation, German Department, Rochester Theological Seminary, 1897–1902; church history, Rochester Theological Seminary, 1902–18. *Christianity and the Social Crisis* (1907); *Prayers of the Social Awakening* (1910); *Christianizing the Social Order* (1912); *The Social Principles of Jesus* (1916); *A Theology for the Social Gospel* (1917).

Sheldon, Charles. Congregationalist. B. Wellsville, N.Y., February 26, 1857; d. February 24, 1946. B.A., Brown University, 1883; graduated, Andover Theological School, 1886. Pastor, Waterbury, Vt., 1886–88; Central Congregational Church, Topeka, Kansas, 1889–1919; editor, *The Christian Herald,* 1920–25. *In His Steps: What Would Jesus Do?* (1896) and other popular novels.

Smith, Gerald Birney. Baptist. B. Middlefield, Mass., May 3, 1868; d. April 3, 1929. B.A., Brown University, 1891; M.A., Columbia, 1898; B.D., Union Theological Seminary, 1898; studied in Berlin, Marburg, and Paris, 1898–1900. Taught Latin, modern languages, and mathematics in preparatory schools, 1891–95; systematic theology, University of Chicago, 1895–1929. *Practical*

Theology (1903); *Social Idealism and the Changing Theology* (1913).

Smyth, (Samuel Phillips) Newman. Congregationalist. B. Brunswick, Maine, June 25, 1843; d. January 6, 1925. B.A., Bowdoin College, 1863, M.A., 1866; graduated Andover Theological School, 1867; studied in Europe, 1868–69. Pastor, Harrison St. Chapel (later Pilgrim Church), Providence, R.I., 1867; First Congregational Church, Bangor, Maine, 1870–75; First Presbyterian Church, Quincy, Ill., 1876–82; First Congregational Church, New Haven, Conn., 1882–1907. *Old Faiths in New Light* (1879); *The Orthodox Theology of Today* (1881); *Through Science to Faith* (1902); *Constructive Natural Theology* (1913).

Williams, Leighton. Baptist, later Episcopalian. B. 1855; d. 1935. Practiced law, then ordained. Pastor, Amity Baptist Church, New York City, thirty years; later, briefly, rector of Episcopal parish. Founder and editor, with Rauschenbusch and others, of *For the Right,* a newspaper for working people, 1889; founder, with Rauschenbusch and Samuel Zane Batten, of the Brotherhood of the Kingdom, 1892. "The Baptist Position: Its Experimental Basis," and other essays.

NOTES

Chapter One

PROLOGUE: THE SHAPE OF THINGS PRESENT

1. Reinhold Niebuhr, *Moral Man and Immoral Society: A Study in Ethics and Politics* (Charles Scribner's Sons, 1932).
2. Wilhelm Pauck, *The Heritage of the Reformation* (Beacon Press, Inc., 1950), p. 280.
3. *Ibid.*, p. 250.
4. *Ibid.*, pp. 281 ff.
5. *Ibid.*, p. 282.
6. *Ibid.*, p. 283.
7. *Ibid.*
8. *Ibid.*, pp. 289–290.
9. *Ibid.*, p. 250.
10. *Ibid.*, p. 278.
11. Wilhelm Pauck, *The Heritage of the Reformation* (The Free Press of Glencoe, 1961), revised and enlarged edition.
12. *Ibid.*, p. 358.
13. Daniel Day Williams, *God's Grace and Man's Hope* (Harper & Brothers, 1949), p. 18.
14. *Ibid.*
15. *Ibid.*, p. 32.
16. *Ibid.*, p. 11.
17. L. Harold DeWolf, *The Case for Theology in the Liberal Perspective* (The Westminster Press, 1959).
18. *Ibid.*, p. 12.
19. Kenneth Cauthen, *The Impact of American Religious Liberalism* (Harper & Brothers, 1961).
20. *Ibid.*, pp. xi–xii.
21. *Ibid.*, p. xii.
22. Friedrich Schleiermacher, *On Religion: Speeches to Its Cultured Despisers,* intro. by Rudolf Otto (Harper & Brothers, 1958).
23. Friedrich Schleiermacher, *The Christian Faith,* intro. by Richard R. Niebuhr (Harper & Row, Publishers, Inc., 1963).
24. Adolf Harnack, *What Is Christianity?* intro. by Rudolf Bultmann (Harper & Brothers, 1957).
25. Adolf Harnack, *The History of Dogma* (Dover Publications, Inc., 1961).

26. Adolf Harnack, *The Mission and Expansion of Christianity in the First Three Centuries,* intro. by Jaroslav Pelikan (Harper & Row, Publishers, Inc., 1962).

27. Ernst Troeltsch, *Christian Thought,* ed. with an intro. by Baron F. von Hügel (Living Age Book, Meridian Books, Inc., 1957).

28. Ernst Troeltsch, *Protestantism and Progress* (Beacon Press, Inc., 1958).

29. Ernst Troeltsch, *The Social Teaching of the Christian Churches,* intro. by H. Richard Niebuhr (Harper & Brothers, 1960).

30. Claude Welch, ed., *God and Incarnation in Mid–Nineteenth Century German Theology* (Oxford University Press, Inc., 1965).

31. H. Shelton Smith, ed., *Horace Bushnell* (Oxford University Press, Inc., 1965).

32. Robert T. Handy, ed., *The Social Gospel in America* (Oxford University Press, Inc., 1966).

33. Albrecht Ritschl, *The Christian Doctrine of Justification and Reconciliation* (Reference Book Publishers, Inc.).

34. Richard R. Niebuhr, *Schleiermacher on Christ and Religion* (Charles Scribner's Sons, 1964).

35. Benjamin A. Reist, *Toward a Theology of Involvement: The Thought of Ernst Troeltsch* (The Westminster Press, 1966).

36. Philip Hefner, *Faith and the Vitalities of History* (Harper & Row, Publishers, Inc., 1966); Peter C. Hodgson, *The Formation of Historical Theology* (Harper & Row, Publishers, Inc., 1966). The volume on Schleiermacher is being prepared by Gerhard Spiegler, the volume on Harnack by G. Wayne Glick.

37. Harnack, *What Is Christianity?* p. viii.

38. Daniel Day Williams, *op. cit.,* p. 22.

39. Newman Smyth, *Old Faiths in New Light* (Charles Scribner's Sons, 1879).

40. H. Shelton Smith, *Changing Conceptions of Original Sin* (Charles Scribner's Sons, 1955), p. 169.

41. Quoted in John Wright Buckham, *Progressive Religious Thought in America* (Houghton Mifflin Company, 1919), p. 268.

42. Theodore Munger, *The Freedom of Faith* (Houghton Mifflin Company, 1883), p. 6.

43. *Ibid.,* p. 25.

44. H. Shelton Smith, *Changing Conceptions of Original Sin,* p. 165.

45. Shailer Mathews, *New Faith for Old* (The Macmillan Company, 1936), pp. 196–197.

46. Walter Rauschenbusch, *A Theology for the Social Gospel* (The Macmillan Company, 1917).

47. Donald Baillie, *God Was in Christ* (Charles Scribner's Sons, 1948), Ch. 5.

48. Definition of mathematical locus in *Webster's Collegiate Dictionary, Fifth Edition* (G. and E. Merriam Co., 1943).

49. H. Richard Niebuhr, *Christ and Culture* (Harper & Brothers, 1956), pp. 43–44.

Chapter Two

LIBERALISM'S THEOLOGICAL HERITAGE: A BRIEF SURVEY

1. Quoted in Hugh Ross Mackintosh, *Types of Modern Theology* (London: James Nisbet & Co., Ltd., 1952), p. 3.
2. *Ibid.,* pp. 3–4.
3. Smyth, *op. cit.,* pp. 159–160.
4. Quoted in Buckham, *op. cit.,* p. 266.
5. D. R. Sharpe, *Walter Rauschenbusch* (The Macmillan Company, 1942), pp. 44–49, 68–69.
6. Donovan Smucker, "The Origins of Walter Rauschenbusch's Social Ethics" (unpublished Ph.D. dissertation, University of Chicago, 1957), pp. 239, 217–225.
7. Rauschenbush, *op. cit.,* n. 139.
8. Smucker, *op. cit.,* p. 228.
9. Cauthen, *op. cit.,* p. 107.
10. *Ibid.,* p. 42.
11. Mathews, *op. cit.,* pp. 42, 44.
12. Cf. Daniel Day Williams, *The Andover Liberals* (Columbia University Press, 1941).
13. Buckham, *op. cit.,* p. 199.
14. *Ibid.,* p. 201.
15. Rauschenbusch, *op. cit.,* n. 139.
16. Smucker, *op. cit.,* p. 245.
17. Rauschenbusch, *op. cit.,* pp. 27–28.
18. *Ibid.,* p. 25.
19. Friedrich Schleiermacher, *The Christian Faith* (Edinburgh: T. & T. Clark, 1928).
20. Mackintosh, *op. cit.,* p. 60.
21. Karl Barth, *From Rousseau to Ritschl* (London: SCM Press, Ltd., 1959).
22. Paul Tillich, *Systematic Theology* (The University of Chicago Press, 1951), Vol. I, p. 41.
23. Schleiermacher, *On Religion,* p. 31.
24. *Ibid.,* pp. 49–50.
25. *Ibid.,* p. 39.
26. *Ibid.,* p. 36.
27. *Ibid.,* pp. 48–49.
28. Schleiermacher, *The Christian Faith,* pp. 132–133.
29. *Ibid.,* p. 283.
30. *Ibid.,* p. 270.
31. *Ibid.,* p. 262.
32. *Ibid.,* p. 385.
33. *Ibid.,* p. 103.
34. *Ibid.,* p. 52
35. Albrecht Ritschl, *The Christian Doctrine of Justification and Reconciliation* (Edinburgh: T. & T. Clark, 1902), Vol. III, p. 10.
36. *Ibid.,* p. 13.

37. *Ibid.*, p. 85.
38. *Ibid.*, p. 13.
39. *Ibid.*, p. 349.
40. *Ibid.*, p. 378.
41. *Ibid.*, p. 383.
42. *Ibid.*
43. *Ibid.*, p. 450.
44. *Ibid.*, p. 406.
45. *Ibid.*, p. 398.
46. *Ibid.*, p. 451.
47. *Ibid.*, p. 406.
48. *Ibid.*, p. 139.
49. *Ibid.*, p. 2.
50. *Ibid.*, p. 38.
51. *Ibid.*, p. 39.
52. Wilhelm Herrmann, *The Communion of the Christian with God* (London, Edinburgh, Oxford: Williams and Norgate, 1895).
53. *Ibid.*, p. 55.
54. *Ibid.*, p. 52.
55. *Ibid.*, p. 63.
56. *Ibid.*, p. 65.
57. *Ibid.*, p. 28.
58. *Ibid.*, p. 61.
59. Harnack, *What Is Christianity?* p. 8.
60. *Ibid.*, p. 51.
61. *Ibid.*, p. 180.
62. *Ibid.*, p. 184.
63. *Ibid.*, p. vii.
64. Mackintosh, *op. cit.*, p. 201.
65. *Ibid.*, pp. 198–200.
66. Troeltsch, *Christian Thought,* "The Place of Christianity Among the World Religions," pp. 50–51. This is Troeltsch's own summary of his point of view in *The Absolute Validity of Christianity.*
67. *Ibid.*, p. 52.
68. *Ibid.*, pp. 55–56.
69. *Ibid.*, p. 53.
70. See H. Richard Niebuhr, *The Meaning of Revelation* (The Macmillan Company, 1941), esp. Ch. 1.
71. Buckham, *op. cit.*, p. 49.
72. In W. G. T. Shedd, ed., *The Complete Works of Samuel Taylor Coleridge* (Harper & Brothers, 1853), Vol. I.
73. Buckham, *op. cit.*, p. 48.
74. Shedd, *op. cit.*, p. 72.
75. *Ibid.*, p. 73.
76. *Ibid.*, p. 74.
77. *Ibid.*, p. 78.
78. *Ibid.*, p. 195.
79. *Ibid.*, p. 196.

80. *Ibid.*, p. 48.
81. *Ibid.*, p. 85.
82. *Ibid.*, p. 247.
83. *Ibid.*
84. *Ibid.*, p. 241.
85. *Ibid.*, p. 246.
86. Samuel Taylor Coleridge, *Confessions of an Inquiring Spirit* (London: Adam and Charles Black, Ltd., 1956), p. 64.
87. *Ibid.*, p. 23. This is the characterization of Coleridge's view by Joseph Henry Green in his introduction to the 1853 edition of the *Confessions.*
88. *Ibid.*, p. 75.
89. Shedd, *op. cit.*, p. 233.
90. H. Richard Niebuhr, *The Kingdom of God in America* (Shoe String Press, Inc., 1956; Harper Torchbook.)
91. H. Richard Niebuhr, *Social Sources of Denominationalism* (Meridian Books, Inc., 1957).
92. Quoted in Niebuhr, *The Kingdom of God in America,* pp. 52–53. Quotations used by permission of Harper & Row, Publishers, Inc.
93. *Ibid.*, p. 69.
94. *Ibid.*, p. 62.
95. Quoted in Niebuhr, *ibid.*, p. 76.
96. *Ibid.*, p. 95.
97. *Ibid.*, p. 109.
98. *Ibid.*, p. 113.
99. *Ibid.*, p. 116.
100. *Ibid.*, pp. 153–154.
101. *Ibid.*, p. 194.
102. *Ibid.*
103. *Ibid.*, p. 184.
104. *Ibid.*, p. 197.
105. Sidney Mead is responsible for the description of Taylor as a "bridge" figure, and I am extending that significance to Bushnell as well.
106. Smith, ed., *Horace Bushnell,* p. 131.
107. *Ibid.*, see selections from *Nature and the Supernatural,* especially pp. 142–151.
108. Westminster Confession, Ch. VI, Sec. 2.
109. *Ibid.*, VI:3.
110. Larger Catechism, Answer to Question 22.
111. *Ibid.*
112. Smith, *Changing Conceptions of Original Sin,* p. 3.
113. *Ibid.*, Ch. 2.
114. *Ibid.*, pp. 82–83.
115. Quoted in Smith, *ibid.*, p. 72.
116. *Ibid.*, especially Chs. 5 and 6.
117. For the material on Taylor, I am primarily indebted to Sidney Mead, *Nathaniel William Taylor, 1786–1858, A Connecticut Liberal* (The

University of Chicago Press, 1942).

118. *Ibid.*, p. 102.
119. *Ibid.*, p. 125.
120. *Ibid.*, p. 111.
121. *Ibid.*, pp. 189–190.
122. *Ibid.*, p. 120.
123. *Ibid.*, pp. 108–109.
124. *Ibid.*, p. 161.
125. *Nature and the Supernatural* in Smith, ed., *Horace Bushnell*, p. 147.
126. *Ibid.*
127. *Ibid.*, p. 151.
128. *Ibid.*, p. 145.
129. *Ibid.*, p. 147.
130. *Christian Nurture* (1861) was one of Bushnell's most influential works.
131. *The Vicarious Sacrifice, Grounded in Principles of Universal Obligation* quoted in H. Shelton Smith, Robert T. Handy, and Lefferts A. Loetscher, *American Christianity* (Charles Scribner's Sons, 1963), Vol. II, p. 273.
132. *Nature and the Supernatural* in Smith, ed., *Horace Bushnell*, p. 139.
133. *The Vicarious Sacrifice*, quoted in Smith, Handy, and Loetscher, *op. cit.*, p. 272.
134. *Ibid.*, p. 273.
135. Quoted in H. R. Heininger, *The Theological Technique of a Mediating Theologian — Horace Bushnell* (privately distributed by the University of Chicago Library, 1935), pp. 163–164.

Chapter Three

A PROFILE OF AMERICAN THEOLOGICAL LIBERALISM, 1879–1917

1. H. R. Niebuhr, *The Kingdom of God in America*, pp. 184–190.
2. *Ibid.*, p. 190.
3. Williams, *God's Grace and Man's Hope*, p. 22.
4. William Newton Clarke, *An Outline of Christian Theology*, Ninth Edition (Edinburgh: T. & T. Clark, 1910), p. 224.
5. *Ibid.*, p. 226.
6. Newell Dwight Hillis, *A Man's Value to Society* (Fleming H. Revell Company), p. 82.
7. *Ibid.*, p. 83.
8. Quoted in W. S. Hudson, *The Great Tradition of the American Churches* (Harper & Brothers, 1953), pp. 174–175.
9. Walter Rauschenbusch, " Religion the Life of God in the Soul of Man " (1900).
10. Munger, *The Freedom of Faith*, p. 27.
11. Shailer Mathews, *The Gospel and the Modern Man* (The Macmillan Company, 1912), p. 43.

12. William Adams Brown, *Modern Theology and the Preaching of the Gospel* (Charles Scribner's Sons, 1914), p. 104.
13. *Ibid.*, p. 123.
14. Hillis, *op. cit.*, p. 101.
15. Henry Ward Beecher, *Evolution and Religion* (Fords, Howard and Hulbert, 1885), p. 79.
16. George A. Gordon, *The New Epoch for Faith* (Houghton Mifflin Company, 1901), p. 12.
17. Munger, *op. cit.*, pp. 12–13.
18. Summarized from Clarke, *op. cit.*, p. 49.
19. Brown, *op. cit.*, p. 104.
20. Summarized from Clarke, *op. cit.*, p. 191.
21. *Ibid.*, p. 397.
22. *Ibid.*, p. 396.
23. William Adams Brown, *Christian Theology in Outline* (Charles Scribner's Sons, 1906), p. 39.
24. Clarke, *op. cit.*, p. 213.
25. Quoted in Hudson, *op. cit.*, p. 183.
26. Clarke, *op. cit.*, p. 245.
27. *Ibid.*, p. 208.
28. *Ibid.*, p. 207.
29. *Ibid.*, pp. 137–138.
30. Rauschenbusch, *A Theology for the Social Gospel,* p. 162.
31. *Ibid.*, pp. 174–175.
32. Mathews, *The Gospel and the Modern Man,* p. 45.
33. George Burman Foster, *The Finality of the Christian Religion* (The University of Chicago Press, 1906), p. 187.
34. *Ibid.*, pp. 480–481.
35. *Ibid.*, p. 405.
36. Brown, *Modern Theology and the Preaching of the Gospel,* Ch. 1.
37. Clarke, *op. cit.*, pp. 11–12.
38. Mathews, *The Gospel and the Modern Man,* p. 64.
39. Foster, *op. cit.*, pp. 404–405.
40. Rauschenbusch, *A Theology for the Social Gospel,* p. 154.
41. *Ibid.*, p. 152.
42. *Ibid.*, 166.
43. *Ibid.*, pp. 150–151.
44. Gordon, *op. cit.*. pp. 390–391.
45. Clarke, *op. cit.*, p. 295.
46. Beecher, *op. cit.*, p. 161.
47. Rauschenbusch, *A Theology for the Social Gospel,* p. 14.
48. Hudson, *op. cit.*, p. 187. The internal quotation is from Gladden, and the setting is Hudson's summary of Gladden's view.
49. Ritschl, *op. cit.*, p. 414.
50. Rauschenbusch, *A Theology for the Social Gospel,* p. 99.
51. *Ibid.*, p. 142.
52. *Ibid.*, p. 140.
53. Mathews, *The Gospel and the Modern Man,* p. 76.

54. Foster, *op. cit.,* p. 472.
55. Gerald Birney Smith, *Social Idealism and the Changing Theology* (The Macmillan Company, 1913), p. 212.
56. See Ralph Gabriel, *The Course of American Democratic Thought* (The Ronald Press Co., 1940), Ch. 13.
57. Quoted in Hudson, *op. cit.,* p. 173.
58. Munger, *op. cit.,* p. 11.
59. *Ibid.,* p. 12.
60. Gordon, *op. cit.,* pp. 3, 6.
61. Hillis, *op. cit.,* p. 102.
62. Brown, *Modern Theology and the Preaching of the Gospel,* p. 105.
63. Mathews, *The Gospel and the Modern Man,* p. 239.
64. Shirley Jackson Case, *The Historical Method in the Study of Religion,* Lewiston, Maine, p. 15.
65. Leighton Williams, "The Baptist Position: Its Experimental Basis," *Amity Tracts,* No. 1 (1892), pp. 12–13.
66. William Newton Clarke, *What Shall We Think of Christianity?* (Charles Scribner's Sons, 1899), p. 116.
67. Walter Rauschenbusch, "The Freedom of Spiritual Religion" (1910), p. 12.
68. Shirley Jackson Case, *The Evolution of Early Christianity* (The University of Chicago Press, 1914), p. 27.
69. Munger, *op. cit.,* p. 18.
70. William Newton Clarke, *Sixty Years with the Bible* (Charles Scribner's Sons, 1910), pp. 157–158.
71. Rauschenbusch, *A Theology for the Social Gospel,* p. 190.
72. Brown, *Modern Theology and the Preaching of the Gospel,* pp. 76 ff.
73. Beecher, *op. cit.,* p. 64.
74. Clarke, *Sixty Years with the Bible,* p. 199.
75. *Ibid.,* pp. 253–254.
76. Brown, *Christian Theology in Outline,* p. 55.
77. Beecher, *op. cit.,* p. 68.
78. Clarke, *An Outline of Christian Theology,* p. 22.
79. Quoted in Buckham, *op. cit.,* pp. 75, 80.
80. Clarke, *What Shall We Think of Christianity?* p. 94.
81. Walter Rauschenbusch, "The Ideals of the Social Reformers," *American Journal of Sociology,* Sept., 1898, pp. 202–203.
82. Gordon, *op. cit.,* p. 387.
83. Quoted in Hudson, *op. cit.,* p. 192.
84. Clarke, *What Shall We Think of Christianity?* p. 94.
85. Mathews, *The Gospel and the Modern Man,* p. 262.
86. Beecher, *op. cit.,* pp. 90–91.
87. Hudson, *op. cit.,* p. 177.
88. *Ibid.,* p. 230.
89. Foster, *op. cit.,* p. xiii.
90. Mathews, *The Gospel and the Modern Man,* p. 7.

91. In Arnold S. Nash, ed., *Protestant Thought in the Twentieth Century* (The Macmillan Company, 1951), p. 228.
92. Clarke, *What Shall We Think of Christianity?* p. 97.
93. Rauschenbusch, *A Theology for the Social Gospel,* p. 12.

Chapter Four

THE VARIETIES OF LIBERALISM: THREE SIGNIFICANT VARIABLES

1. Unpublished lectures at the University of Chicago.
2. William Newton Clarke, *An Outline of Christian Theology* (Edinburgh: T. & T. Clark, 1901), p. 12.
3. *Ibid.,* p. 5.
4. Rauschenbusch, " Religion the Life of God in the Soul of Man," *loc. cit.,* p. 7.
5. Shailer Mathews, " A Positive Method for an Evangelical Theology," *American Journal of Theology,* January, 1909, p. 22.
6. Mathews, *The Gospel and the Modern Man,* p. 92.
7. George Burman Foster, " Christianity and Modern Culture," *American Journal of Theology,* January, 1909, p. 148.
8. Douglas Clyde Macintosh, *Christianity in Its Modern Expression* (The Macmillan Company, 1921), p. 76.
9. H. Richard Niebuhr, *The Kingdom of God in America,* p. 194.
10. Rauschenbusch, *A Theology for the Social Gospel,* p. 32.
11. *Ibid.,* p. 57.
12. *Ibid.,* p. 59.
13. *Ibid.,* pp. 57–58.
14. Clarke, *An Outline of Christian Theology,* p. 230.
15. Brown, *Christian Theology in Outline,* p. 269.
16. Rauschenbusch, *A Theology for the Social Gospel,* p. 99.
17. *Ibid.,* p. 97.
18. *Ibid.,* p. 100.
19. Clarke, *An Outline of Christian Theology,* p. 279.
20. Rauschenbusch, *A Theology for the Social Gospel,* p. 152.
21. Clarke, *An Outline of Christian Theology,* pp. 369, 370.
22. Rauschenbusch, *A Theology for the Social Gospel,* p. 193.
23. See the studies of Brown in Smith, *Changing Conceptions of Original Sin,* Ch. 8, and Kenneth Cauthen, *The Impact of American Religious Liberalism,* Ch. 3.
24. D. C. Macintosh and others, *Religious Realism* (The Macmillan Company, 1931), p. 326.
25. *Ibid.,* p. 399.
26. *Ibid.,* p. 375.
27. Summarized in James A. Martin, *Empirical Philosophies of Religion* (King's Crown Press, 1945), p. 75.
28. D. C. Macintosh, *The Problem of Religious Knowledge* (Harper & Brothers, 1940), Ch. 12.
29. *Ibid.,* p. 360.

30. Martin, *op. cit.*, p. 74.
31. George F. Thomas, "The Philosophy of Religion," in Nash, ed., *op. cit.*, p. 83.
32. Shailer Mathews, *The Faith of Modernism* (The Macmillan Company, 1924). For what follows, see especially Chs. 1 and 2.
33. Shailer Mathews, *Contributions of Science to Religion* (Appleton-Century-Crofts, Inc., 1924). For what follows, see especially Chs. 15–18.
34. *Ibid.*, p. 385.
35. *Ibid.*, p. 377.
36. Shailer Mathews, "The Social Origins of Theology," *The American Journal of Sociology*, Vol. XVIII, No. 3 (November, 1912), p. 289.
37. *Ibid.*, p. 294.
38. *Ibid.*, p. 316.
39. *Ibid.*, p. 317.
40. Mathews, *New Faith for Old*, pp. 69–70.
41. For a study of key figures in the liberal movement, 1900–1935, including Fosdick, see Cauthen, *op. cit.*
42. H. Richard Niebuhr, *The Kingdom of God in America*, p. 194.
43. For a more complete description of this movement, see especially Gabriel, *op. cit.*, upon which this section on accommodationism depends.
44. Quoted in Gabriel, *op. cit.*, pp. 150–151. Emphasis supplied.
45. *Ibid.*, p. 151.
46. *Ibid.*, p. 152.
47. *Ibid.*, pp. 151–152.
48. *Ibid.*, p. 149.
49. *Ibid.*
50. *Ibid.*, pp. 149–150.
51. *Ibid.*, p. 156.
52. Walter Rauschenbusch, *Christianity and the Social Crisis* (The Macmillan Company, 1913), p. 47.
53. *Ibid.*, p. 48.
54. *Ibid.*, p. 65.
55. *Ibid.*, p. 67.
56. Rauschenbusch, *A Theology for the Social Gospel*, p. 183.
57. Rauschenbusch, *Christianity and the Social Crisis*, p. 67.
58. *Ibid.*, p. 71.
59. Rauschenbusch, *A Theology for the Social Gospel*, p. 184.
60. Walter Rauschenbusch, *Christianizing the Social Order* (The Macmillan Company, 1912), pp. 321–322.
61. Rauschenbusch, *A Theology for the Social Gospel*, p. 3.
62. Shailer Mathews, *The Church and the Changing Order* (The Macmillan Company, 1912), p. 128.
63. *Ibid.*, p. 140.
64. *Ibid.*, p. 142.
65. *Ibid.*, p. 145.
66. *Ibid.*, p. 168.
67. *Ibid.*, pp. 165–166.
68. *Ibid.*, p. 171.

69. *Ibid.*, p. 179.
70. Winthrop S. Hudson, " Walter Rauschenbusch and the New Evangelism," *Religion in Life,* Vol. XXX, No. 3 (1961), p. 417.
71. Rauschenbusch, *Christianizing the Social Order,* p. 334.
72. Shailer Mathews, *The French Revolution 1789–1815* (Longmans, Green & Co., Inc., 1924), p. 446. Emphasis supplied.
73. W. S. Hudson, *American Protestantism* (The University of Chicago Press, 1961), p. 141.
74. Mathews, *New Faith for Old,* pp. 69–70.

Chapter Five
EPILOGUE: THE SHAPE OF THINGS TO COME

1. Roy A. Burkhart, " Toward a Healthy Theology," *The Christian Century,* Dec. 19, 1956.
2. *Ibid.*, p. 1478.
3. *Ibid.*, p. 1480.
4. *Ibid.*, pp. 1478–1479.
5. *Ibid.*, pp. 1478, 1480.
6. *Ibid.*, p. 1479.
7. *Ibid.*
8. Shailer Mathews, ed., *Contributions of Science to Religion,* p. 392.
9. W. Paul Jones, *The Recovery of Life's Meaning* (Association Press, 1963), pp. 93–94.
10. Reinhold Niebuhr, *op. cit.*, p. ix.
11. *Ibid.*, pp. xi–xii.
12. Burkhart, *op. cit.*, pp. 1478–1479.
13. Harvey Cox, *The Secular City* (The Macmillan Company, 1965), p. 105.
14. *Ibid.*, p. 116.
15. *Ibid.*, p. 112.
16. *Ibid.*, p. 113.
17. *Ibid.*
18. *Ibid.*, p. 112.
19. Dietrich Bonhoeffer, *Letters and Papers from Prison* (London: Fontana Books, 1959), p. 91.
20. *Ibid.*, p. 92.
21. Karl Barth, *Church Dogmatics,* I/1 (Edinburgh: T. & T. Clark, 1956), pp. 280–361.
22. Richard R. Niebuhr, " A Power and a Goodness," *The Christian Century,* Dec. 1, 1965, p. 1473.
23. Langdon Gilkey, " Dissolution and Reconstruction in Theology," *The Christian Century,* Feb. 3, 1965, p. 137.
24. Charles Long, " Homo Religiosus: The Perennial Human Type," *Religion on Campus,* Spring, 1966, p. 12.
25. Gilkey, *loc. cit.*
26. Barth, *From Rousseau to Ritschl,* p. 353.
27. Van Harvey, " The Nature and Function of Faith," *The Christian Century,* Aug. 4, 1965, p. 963.

28. *Ibid.*, pp. 963–964.
29. *Ibid.*, p. 963.
30. Richard R. Niebuhr, *loc. cit.*, p. 1474.
31. *Ibid.*, p. 1473.
32. Schubert M. Ogden, "Faith and Truth," *The Christian Century*, Sept. 1, 1965, p. 1059.
33. *Ibid.*
34. *Ibid.*, p. 1060.
35. Van Harvey, *loc. cit.*, p. 964
36. *Ibid.*
37. Gilkey, loc. cit., p. 137.
38. John B. Cobb, Jr., "Christian Natural Theology and Christian Existence," *The Christian Century*, March 3, 1965, p. 266.
39. Ogden, *op. cit.*, p. 1060.
40. William H. Hamilton, "The New Optimism—from Ringo to Prufrock," in Thomas J. J. Altizer and William Hamilton, *Radical Theology and the Death of God* (The Bobbs-Merrill Company, Inc., 1966), p. 159.
41. *Ibid.*, p. 158.
42. *Ibid.*, p. 161.
43. *Ibid.*, p. 162.
44. *Ibid.*, p. 164.
45. *Ibid.*, p. 167.
46. *Ibid.*, p. 168.
47. *Ibid.*, p. 169.
48. Harvey Cox, "The Place and Purpose of Theology," *The Christian Century*, Jan. 5, 1966, p. 7.
49. Cox, *The Secular City*, p. 121.
50. *Ibid.*, p. 123.
51. Gibson Winter, *The New Creation as Metropolis* (The Macmillan Company, 1963), pp. 2–3.
52. John A. T. Robinson, *Honest to God* (The Westminster Press, 1963), p. 115.
53. Reinhold Niebuhr, *An Interpretation of Christian Ethics* (Harper & Brothers, 1935), p. 111.
54. Joseph Fletcher, *Situation Ethics: The New Morality* (The Westminster Press, 1966), pp. 61–62.
55. *Ibid.*, pp. 143–144.
56. William Hamilton, "The Death of God," *Playboy*, Aug. 1966, p. 139.
57. William Hamilton, *The New Essence of Christianity* (Association Press, 1961), pp. 89–91.
58. *Ibid.*, pp. 90–91.
59. Cox, "The Place and Purpose of Theology," *loc. cit.*, p. 8.
60. *Ibid.*, p. 9.
61. Gilkey, *op. cit.*, p. 38.
62. *Ibid.*
63. H. Richard Niebuhr, *The Kingdom of God in America*, p. 194.

Appendix

BIOGRAPHICAL NOTES

1. This appendix has been compiled, in part, with the help of the following biographical sources: *Who Was Who in America,* Historical Volume 1607–1896, Volume I 1897–1942 (A. N. Marquis Company, 1963, 1941); *The Dictionary of American Biography* (Charles Scribner's Sons, 1935); *The Twentieth Century Encyclopedia of Religious Knowledge* (Baker Book House, 1955); and John Wright Buckham, *Progressive Religious Thought in America* (Houghton Mifflin Company, 1919). Information on Leighton Williams was provided by Edward Starr, Curator, Samuel Colgate Baptist Historical Collection, Rochester, New York.

INDEX